LOVE AND LAW IN EUROPE

Love and Law in Europe

Edited by

HANNE PETERSEN

Routledge
Taylor & Francis Group
LONDON AND NEW YORK

First published 1998 by Dartmouth and Ashgate Publishing

Reissued 2018 by Routledge
2 Park Square, Milton Park, Abingdon, Oxon, OX14 4RN
52 Vanderbilt Avenue, New York, NY 10017

Routledge is an imprint of the Taylor & Francis Group, an informa business

A Library of Congress record exists under LC control number: 97041411

ISBN 13: 978-1-138-36176-8 (hbk)
ISBN 13: 978-0-429-43242-2 (ebk)

Acknowledgement is made of permission to reprint, without notes, pages 212-218 from Saxo Grammaticus. The History of the Danes, Vol 1. Translated by Peter Fisher. Edited by Hilda Ellis Davidson. By permission of D.S. Brewer, Rowman and Littlefield.

Contents

Introduction

This book is the result of support, inspiration, interest and cooperation of both the authors of the articles presented here and of other colleagues and friends without whom this anthology would never have been produced.

I have worked with issues concerning love and law since 1992, originally inspired and puzzled particularly by two observations.

The first observation was that although the Rome Treaty and the 1989 treaty on the social dimensions of the European Community would guarantee freedom of mobility for labourers in Europe, the statistics seemed to show that very few persons who were citizens of the memberstates actually moved. My superficial observations of people's motivations for movement seemed to indicate that love relations presented as much of an attraction for movement as did work relations - at least in the case of a 'peripheral' EU-country as Denmark. However the power of love to move people had not received much attention in jurisprudential theory not to speak of legal protection.

The second observation was that during the drawn out processes of the two well-known Danish referenda on the Maastricht treaties in 1992 and 1993 there was discussion of what seemed as lack of political and emotional support for the European Union amongst especially Danish women. A female 'passion of Europeanism' seemed weak, but there certainly were strongly held emotions and passions among both men and women related to the development of and further integration of a European community and union by legal means.

There were also discussions about the non-rational and supposedly rather emotional character of the votes cast during the referenda. Several politicians and journalists expressed views about the irrational and even ignorant and irresponsible electorate. But this first referendum also was a very powerful example and a lesson about the political importance of public sentiment. A sentiment which had thus far been either ignored or expected to change due to information and rational arguments from politicians and legal, economic and other experts in the field. These arguments proved not to have the expected effect, however, and the often quite arrogant attitude was modified, and public opinion and sentiment received far more political attention than before.[1]

These political and legal developments seemed to arouse passions which neither lawyers (nor politicians) nor the general public knew very well how to deal with. Theories about legal positivism have had a strong impact on the understanding of law both amongst professionals and societies at large at least in Denmark and the Nordic countries. As is well known these theories have underlined the impassionate, general, 'rational', and 'objective' character of modern law. Recent developments indicate that these views are gradually changing in many European countries. We are perhaps witnessing a real crisis of 'modern' positivist legal thinking and of the authority which this thinking and the legal systems have had in Europe.

Luisa Passerini in her article in this volume on 'Love and Europe. Cultural Trends in the 1930s', writes that assumptions in Europe that claimed especially romantic love as a certain privileged European sentiment have been rejected by anthropological research. That love can no longer (if it ever could) be seen as a specifically European sentiment forming the basis of human community is demonstrated clearly in the articles by Marie-Claire Foblets and Thomas Spijkerboer in this volume, which deal with legal consequences of love relations between so called third country nationals or 'immigrants' and EU-citizens.

That (modern) law is a supreme instrument to create order in human societies was perhaps also if not a European then a Western understanding that we may have to revise. We should however not forget that love is certainly a force which also moves Europeans both physically and psychically. Furthermore we should not overlook the fact that much emotional and intellectual energy as well as economic expenditure has been invested in the creation and refinement of the instrument of modern legislation and in attempts to make this instrument also work on a supranational level.

To deal with such 'esoteric' and so far almost uncultivated topics as love and law, situated at the fringe or periphery of modern jurisprudence, or belonging to the 'minor jurisprudences' in Peter Goodrich's terms,[2] has required both emotional, intellectual and practical support which I have been so fortunate also to receive.

In a way I have sometimes felt that I have not really chosen to deal with this topic. Once I had opened up Pandora's box of gifts and enigmas, and presented some of the findings, I almost felt forced to continue to work on them.

The amount of the support I have received has actually surprised me, and seems to me to indicate that there existed a certain need for cultivation of these issues both across gender, nationality, and political and professional affiliations. Could it perhaps be that the 'Zeitgeist', the spirit of this time and period, longs for other explanations, other combinations and other perspectives than those which have been predominant at least in Europe for half a century or more?

During a yearlong stay at the European University Institute I was encouraged in this work by Yota Kravaritou, who many years ago inspired me by her boldness to speak about emotions in a large conference on labour law. The opportunity to discuss with Luisa Passerini, also at the EUI, her research project on 'Fragments of a history of the love discourse' was another inspiration.

After returning to the faculty of law at the University of Copenhagen I received strong support for the idea of organizing a seminar about 'Love and Law in Europe' as part of the 'Copenhagen Cultural University' to take place during 1996, where Copenhagen was cultural city of Europe. This intellectual, practical and emotional support came especially from my colleague, historian Henrik Stevnsborg. Further important support, not the least financial security, was provided by the Dean of the Faculty of Natural Sciences, Henrik Jeppesen, who was in charge of the Cultural University events. Without their backing the seminar which provided the lectures which have turned into articles for this anthology would not have taken place. As I had in September 1995 moved outside Europe, though not totally outside the realm of European influence, to the University of Greenland in Nuuk, we had to develop a concept for long distance communication and organization.

The enthusiastic support and the ideas of Marie-Claire Foblet for the content of the seminar were inspiring, and the willingness and interest of speakers to participate was very encouraging.

The idea to use a literary text dealing with issues concerning love and law as a common reading and background for the speakers at the conference was Luisa Passerini's. Since the seminar took place in Copenhagen I decided to use the tale about 'Hagbard and Signe', one of the most beloved tales of Danish medieval literature written around the year 1200 - a tale of tragic love and marriage - with close similarities to the problems treated in Tristan and Isolde and Romeo and Juliet.

The contemporary relevance of the problematic of these stories is demonstrated by the immense popularity of performances of Romeo and

Juliet in theatre and film.

All of the articles in this volume except two were originally written for the Copenhagen seminar. The two exceptions are the articles by Luisa Passerini and myself, which were written for a workshop held in Florence in October 1996 on the 'Role of Love in Western Tradition'. This workshop was organized by Luisa Passerini, but as both of us participated in both seminars they have been included in this volume.

As is demonstrated by the articles here the field of love and law is a complex and tangled field, which has remained uncultivated for a very long period especially by lawyers. It is perhaps significant that the lawyers who have found it worthwhile to spend time on disentangling and recultivating the field are lawyers dealing with philosophy of law and legal theory, legal history and immigration law. The other contributors are historians, including a historian of religion and a training analyst and professor of psychology.

I do not think that it is possible to draw any general or strict conclusions on the relations between love and law based upon the articles presented here. My personal view is that these fields, which have long been considered irreconcilable and apart, belonging to a world of reason and a world of emotions respectively, can no longer be held apart, because realities bring them together once again. In this I disagree with some of the authors here.

Maybe we have to move to the supranational field as the European Union (or to the sub-national field as home ruled Greenland and the many other present or future home ruled or locally governed areas or regions inside and outside Europe) to again encounter the links between emotions and communities to be established and protected by law. Hopefully we may also avoid too many examples of the importance of these links leading to or being followed by brutality and violence.

Maybe we have to again experience the obstacles for love relations stemming from irreconcilable ties to and membership of different global 'tribes' or 'dynasties' - ties which in a modern and post-modern world are also established by legal means and not only by bloodlines.

We are moving towards a world where communities change, where modern distinctions between what belongs to a 'public' sphere and what to a 'private' sphere are changing. Changes are taking place in 'production', in the creation and perception of 'politics' and in the constitution of intimate life. National relations, class relations, political organization, gender relations, generational relations, ethnic relations, for a period of time were seemingly stable relations which allowed (not only) legal professionals to take certain emotions so for granted that they were ignored and left to the so-called subjective sciences.

If we are now moving towards a century that may have to reconcile the 'subjective' and the 'objective' to recreate order and to secure reasonably attractive, fulfilling and just relations and communities, that will generate new challenges also for Europe and its inhabitants.

Notes:

1 My earlier publications on this topic include: 'Sociale Dimensioner, køn og kærlighed.' (Social Dimensions, Gender and Love) In *Årsberetning 1992*, Studier no. 50. Retsvidenskabeligt Institut B, University of Copenhagen 1993.
'On Love and Law in European Community Building'. In *Journal of Behavioural and Social Sciences*. Tokai University. Special Issue: Nation Building and Sub-cultures, 1994.
'Informal Law and/of Love in the European Community'. Chapter in *Home Knitted Law. Norms and Values in Gendered Rule-Making*. Dartmouth, Socio-Legal Studies, 1996.

2 Peter Goodrich (1996): *Law in the Courts of Love. Literature and Other Minor Jurisprudences. Routledge.*

The Language of Emotions in the Language of Law

HANNE PETERSEN

'I feel that to allow all passion to be absorbed by the Nation can prove no more than an emergency measure'
(Denis de Rougemont 1983, p.270)

The following article is based upon a number of assumptions. I assume that we are in a period of changes of both emotionality, sites of emotional experience, and order.[1] This raises questions such as where we encounter languages of emotions, and what are their contemporary expressions, forms and sites.

I assume that there are languages - in the plural - of emotions, as it is also my assumption that there are languages - in the plural - of law. I also assume that we will have to deal with issues about order and law in much more diverse and complex ways in the future, one of them perhaps concerning relations between love and justice.

Emotions and order

Emotions and order or law have generally been understood as opposites in modernity. My claim here is that this understanding of emotions and order as juxtapositions - as almost generally excluding each other - is no longer valid. I base this claim upon an understanding of order and law as different from the positivist understanding of law as primarily legislation (Gesetz).

I also base it upon an understanding of emotions as being of both individual and social importance, and thus also of importance for contemporary social or socio-psychic order. Emotions may threaten and support social order. They may perhaps thus also create order and give meaning to actions and relations. Emotions - as law - have consequences in and for social life. They are forces and forms of knowledge that direct and guide both human thought and human action. They connect persons to each other, and thus create communities. Feelings - and among them moral feelings - are connecting linkages of communities, and constitute ordering behaviour in communities.

As the initial citation of de Rougemont indicates, in the modern nation state emotions were almost solely directed - at least legitimately - towards the nation. *'(A) nation requires, that passion shall be translated to the level of the people as a whole' (de Rougemont 1983, p.250).* Also the generation of law and order was almost translated to and identified with the level of the nation. The nation and its institutions, especially the national legislative body, has been understood to be the prime producer of law, and perhaps also of the most important framework of order. This has had emotional implications, as the emotions which have been nationally sustained and promoted through legislation, the executive and the judiciary, have been emotions directed towards the nation.

In the situation we are witnessing in the Western world and in Europe, nation states are being reshuffled and their emotional underpinnings are to some extent disintegrating and being loosened. Former legitimate demands for emotional loyalty against the nations and concomitant legal instruments for the guarantee of this loyalty, such as requirements that 'civil servants' should be national citizens, are now within the EU almost becoming discriminatory acts violating the prohibition against 'national discrimination'.

Emotionality as law or order are relational phenomena. If we want to look for areas or sites where emotions and order meet and interact, we should perhaps not so much look to the language of legislation as to languages of normativity in a broader sense.

Sites of emotions and relations of emotional importance are also sites of normative and legal importance. Denzin, who aims at understanding emotion in the postmodern period mentions as sites of emotional experience the following: home, work, leisure, sexuality, sport, medicine, prisons, film, music, literature, television, schools, church, the court system (Denzin 1990, p.94).

Several of these sites will be important fields of study of the interaction between languages of emotions and languages of law. We are witnessing transitions of both emotional and legal relations. Emotions are being reoriented towards other sites than the nation and order is being created through other means than modern national legislation.

This may lead to a number of rendezvous and conflicts between emotions and legal cultures and perhaps to a more common language of emotions and order.

Languages of emotion

A Danish professor of psychology who has lectured widely for lay audiences and written a recent book on emotions (Johansen 1994), claims that there is a lack of names or terms for emotions. The Danish language is poor in its ability to describe the variety of existing emotions. I wonder if that could be linked to the tendency in modernity to focus strongly on rationality and to suppress all other emotions but national or nationally oriented emotions. The examples, Johansen uses in his book, are almost all from literature and movies. The written and spoken languages of modern sciences including jurisprudence have rarely sought to express the complexity of emotions which have rather been considered anathema for scientific thinking.

It is well known that the novel was highly normative in matters concerning love relations especially in the 19th Century. But also relations between music, musical expressions and emotions were well-known and strong. The importance of the opera seems especially notable here both for the use of the national (Italian) language and for the expression of emotions and notions of class, race and gender in the 20th century (Nousiainen 1993; Susan McClary 1991).

Languages of emotions in the 21st Century will probably be even less exclusively in writing and may become even more visually and tonally or musically oriented due to technological and communicational developments than has been the case at the end of the 20th Century.

Susanne Langer writes that music may articulate forms which language (spoken or written) may not put forward. Music articulates emotions without linking itself decisively to them (Langer 1969).

This ability of music has of course been used in the expression and promotion of national emotions and national anthems, and its use for the creation of supranational emotional expressions is portrayed in the film 'Blue', one of the films in Kieslowski's interesting post-national film trilogy, dealing with both love, and law, dissolution and transition of nation states and emergence of new emotional sites. (Kieslowski's other film in the trilogy 'Red' interestingly also deals with both love and law, this time however closely linked to chance and fate. 'White' seems to deal more with the collapse of law and order and the increasing importance of other relations).

Musical genres such as jazz, rock'n roll, and lately world music, and their public performances on an increasingly large and trans-national scale have undoubtedly contributed to the creation of important sites of emotional experience, and development of generational and trans-national self-consciousness. The festival culture and community is perhaps an example of a postmodern, temporary but nonetheless important emotional experience of community - as are the sports events and the concomitant communities.

A recent trend of combining globally televised, international sports events with musical events is perhaps a sign of a need for intensification and amplification of emotional sites and emotional and moral feelings and expressions beyond and/or below the national realm. The French-Canadian chanteuse, Céline Dion, opened the 1996 Atlanta Olympic Games backed by a 300-member gospel choir. The Cuban-American Gloria Estefan closed it.

On August 12 1996 The Time carried a cover story on 'The Divas of Pop' commenting among others on this event and giving an explanation of why these events had to be presented by such divas, (which Time explains means goddesses) who seem to best embody the professed idealism of the Olympics.

> *'These slots simply had to go to divas. Guys can put across songs of misery and destruction; inspirational paeans are girls stuff. So are role-model personas consistent with the idealism the Olympics try to embody, or at least sell. What male singer could deliver the first song's potent potentially risible message ('And since the dawn of man/The strength of just 'I can'/Has brought together people of all nations') with Dion's strong voice, clear heart and straight face? Who but Estefan, brave survivor of a 1990 bus crash that broke her back, could give such autobiographical grit to her song of resilience? 'So I'll go the distance this time' she intones, 'Seeing more the higher I climb' (Time August 12, 1996).*

The success of opera and musicals perhaps also demonstrates the demand for combinations of visual and tonal forms of expressions of emotions.

The emotional - and normative - importance of movies, of motion pictures, has also been well known in the 20th Century. This century has to a very great degree been the century of films and the film media first in the United States but also in the Western World. If my information is correct, the American film industry has been closely scrutinized by the US Foreign Department.

India is supposed to have the world's biggest film industry today. However in a European context as well as probably in a Latin American one, the impact of the film industry that is felt is the American one. The European home market for films has become American property, and the conflicts during the GATT negotiations a few years ago about the film industry demonstrate the importance of visual media and normativity both in economic and cultural terms (Honoré 1994, p.55).

It is the American film industry which has produced normative images not just for Americans but increasingly for the world. However also in this field the future might prove more complex.

Denzin suggests that the postmodern politics of emotionality locates key emotional feelings in cultural texts that lie outside the person (Denzin, p.105).

> *'Films are simultaneously visual records of, and a part of, everyday life. These records and representations structure lived experience: they set fashion, keep tradition alive, record tabooed acts, and ceremonialize the sacred.. Films are interactional productions. They do not simply assert their truths, 'rather we interact with them in order to arrive at conclusions'.. Film expresses particular versions of the social imagination. Not only do films represent what is 'immediately apparent in a given society'.., but they also allow 'the needs, desires and dreams of a period to be projected' into the realms of the social..'*
> *(Denzin p.102)*

The visual language draws upon and presents emotions. It is also highly normative. I have written on visual normativity in other articles (Petersen 1996, and forthcoming), where I have claimed that visual media is relatively easily accessible, as it does not require literacy, which most people in the world do not acquire until they reach a certain age, and many especially women do never acquire[2]. It may be consumed collectively - and thus can give collective emotional experiences. It therefore seems an almost ideal tool for this purpose of creating an imagined global community - parallelling Anderson's claims that the print media created the imagined national community - for which written law was such an important regulatory instrument (Anderson 1985).

In my opinion films and visual norms through their strong combinations of the emotional and the normative, are very likely to become a much more 'powerful' form of normative communication in today's world than are written forms of communication and among them written laws. Lawyers as professional 'norm-makers' and 'norms-interpreters', should pay much more attention to the messages and morals conveyed by the visual images by which we are surrounded.

Languages of law

What I have claimed above is that we can no longer in the postmodern post-national period distinguish so strongly between the expressions of emotions and the expressions of norms and normativity, and leave emotions for literature, film and music, and reason for jurisprudence.

The language of modern law has been written, and legislation has been considered its most prominent form. In a way it is and has been a very odd form - neither prose nor poetry, with elements of both, but with very restricted regard for aesthetic qualities of legal texts and perhaps especially legislations. But the nation state and the national parliament is no longer understood as the most important context of the creation of 'law'. Perhaps this is also part of the lack of emotional interest and appeal of national parliaments. Discourses on legal pluralism, legal cultures and soft law as well as on human rights conventions and other international conventions, and the growing role of courts in creation of norms demonstrate a shifting understanding of the concept of law not to speak of 'order' which has perhaps been less discussed in legal theory.

It is my claim that the languages of law we are seing already and will be seeing in the future in post-modern societies - both Western and non-Western - will be both written, visual, and oral. I will also claim that the language of law is becoming 'factual' - not in the sense (only) of 'might is right' so that demonstrations of might become right, but rather in the sense, that in periods of transition, acts as such become normative without necessarily being expressed as norms in oral form - as actual and factual examples to be followed, or as acts, which when analyzed, display normative patterns (Petersen 1996).

The contents of these languages or signs, will be broader and encompass both sense and sensibility, reason and vision or emotion.

The Human Rights Conventions are perhaps the most well known international examples of legal texts which do not distinguish so strongly between the language of morality and the professed objective language of law.

The very condensed language also of modern law and legislation, with need of intense and professional interpretation, has similarities with religious and poetic texts. And in Islamic societies which follow the Quran, law is still religious poetry.

It seems that similar phenomena may be observed in premodern Western societies - and that there is thus also a Western tradition of closer linkages between emotionality and order to build upon.

It is often argued that we are approaching another 'middle age'. This claim is advocated specifically on the basis of the strong prominence of visuality in the contemporary world (Lindhardt 1993). Lindhardt (a Danish theologian) asserts that in Medieval times the present clear separation of fact and fiction was lacking.

Everything was considered factual, relating to some kind of reality, embedded in another perception of space and of time than the one which is now dominant. Pictorial 'illustration' was not representation, but rather valuation. Where modernity depicts differences in size the Medieval artist would depict differences of value. Medieval perception was symbolic and narrative mediation, where modern perception became rational and gave priority to correctness and elevation. The oral culture is extrovert and emotional, whereas emotions become more internalized in a literal culture (Lindhardt 1993).

When turning to Western history, to find examples of norms dealing with emotions, I shall mention just a few examples related to the general topic of this paper. The first example is from the old Norse poem 'Havamal' from between 800 - 1200 a.c., which contains 'rules of etiquette' especially the etiquette concerning the importance of friendship.

The tree at the croft dries out
shielded by neither bark nor fir
thus also him, whom nobody loves
wherefore shall he live long
(My translation)

Octavio Paz writes about etiquette that it is never explicit or literal, but rather tacit. As such it faithfully represents the social order. It plays especially with the values of the unspoken, the implicit and the understood.

'Like morality and law, etiquette draws strict boundaries and legislates what can and cannot be done. It never says no, however; rather only this far. And only this far based on conditions that are implicit, not expressed' (Paz 1988, p.188).

The second example is from a compact disc called 'Love's Illusion' by the female vocal group, Anonymous 4, who sings Medieval music. The following example in the English translation is from the Montpellier Codex from the 13th Century. As Ditlev Tamm mentions in his article in this volume the 12th Century was regarded as both the century of romantic love and the Bologna school of Jurisprudence,

> *'for without a sweetheart no one can know right thinking or courtesy or have great joy or feel his heart come alive at all'*

The linking of the sweetheart and the right thinking is what Paul Tillich might call a linking of love and justice, to which I will return later.

What I want to demonstrate with these two superficial quotes is that the dominant western modern understanding that love is the negation of law, as love is partial, particular, involved, whereas law is expected to be objective, general, and detached, is to my view exactly a historically modern one, which assumes a particular understanding of law, and probably also of love. Koen Raes and Emilios Christodoulidis in their articles here argue that love and law have been incommensurable discourses and should also stay separa-te. I no longer agree on the first point, even if it was my initial starting point when I started dealing with issues about love and law. I do not think I agree on the second point either, especially since I do not consider it neither possible nor desirable any longer to keep these discourses apart.

Positivist legal language has claimed objectivity, generality and detachment, but as already mentioned it has not totally banished or ex-patriated emotions, it has reserved and protected them for the national community and for national relations only. Other emotions and loyalties - especially in relation to competitive communities such as families or clans - were discredited and excluded during this process, and one of the means for this was the legal creation of individuals and individual citizens (Kosseleck 1981), and perhaps also the support of individual love as means of creation of relation between gendered individuals.

I am not claiming that written norms will become obsolete, nor am I claiming any identity of the written and the visual norms - they have different forms, are generated differently and have different audiences. And I do not want to claim either that we will only see odd mixtures of normativity and emotionality in the coming millenium.

But I think it is certainly worthwhile to consider whether a visual language of norms and normative visual cultures may be taking over some of the important functions carried out by the written normative culture - creating a minimum of common considerations, values and demands.

If such a change is taking place, it is furthermore relevant to consider its (many) implications - be it from a gender, race, class, ecological or other angle.

Modern lawyers of modern developed nation states have been trained to read and interpret texts, and words, and have acquired elaborate skills in this respect. We have, however, very little training in 'reading' visual languages: images, signs and symbols.

If it is a sufficiently convincing argument that visual and other non-written norms will come to form an important normative communication in the global village it becomes important to study the generation of these norms, their form, their implementation and intention, their content and their audiences.

Film culture is seldom (only) national culture. Visual normativity thus does not necessarily confer 'national' norms, but something broader. Some visual norms are generated by the 'market', by private enterprise, and not by democratic (national) institutions - they are expressions of commercial cultural norms.

Other visual norms are created - and partly financed - by national, supranational or local institutions or organizations, and thus present perhaps different norms and address different audiences for the purpose of conveying normative influences.[3]

Neither written laws nor moving pictures are actual action, but both intend to influence action, however in quite different ways. Modern democracies seek to enforce the 'rule of law'. Law is supposed to be something which governs. It is implemented by way of hierarchically organized public bureaucracies, and enforced through the use of sanctions, the ultimate sanction being physical violence.[4]

The 'implementation' of the motion pictures takes place through mimesis - through the imitation of action or of praxis, rather than through the imperative command of democratic institutions:

> *'the mimetic act is the incarnation into actuality of what we can grasp of reality; which is the reason why we pay enormous salaries and devotion in Hollywood.*
> *(Blackmur 1956, p.187).*

These mimetic norms may be likened more to the 'rule of the game' than to 'imperative' law, about which Hannah Arendt writes that 'the point of these rules is not that I submit to them voluntarily or recognize theoretically their validity, but that in practice I cannot enter the game unless I conform; my motive for acceptance is my wish to play, and since men exist only in the plural, my wish to play is identical with my wish to live.... All laws are "directives' rather than 'imperatives". They direct human intercourse as rules direct the game' (Arendt 1970, p.97).

Languages of emotions in languages of law - on the relation between love and justice

Modern law was not antithetical to emotions. I agree with Rougemont, that all emotions were absorbed by the nation, and that this is a situation which is unstable and also proved to be both destructive and dangerous. Maurizio Viroli,[5] the author of a book called 'For Love of Country', claims that 'love of country can be generous, compassionate, and intelligent, but can also be exclusive, deaf, and blind' (Viroli 1995, p.6). He argues for another understanding of love of country:

> *'One must find ways of encouraging and sustaining the right sort of passions and love; one must enter into the dangerous world of particularity and confront the dangers of exclusive and intolerant loves. Civic virtue has to be particularistic to be possible and yet we do not want it to be dangerous or repugnant'.*
> *(p.12)*

The love he discusses is not the romantic love between man and woman, which Rougemont claimed was specific for the Western world. I do not think that there is any doubt that the 'emotional site' of love between adults - be they of different or same sex - has become again a field where emotions and law meet - perhaps especially so, when lovers come from different parts of the world, nations or political unions as is increasingly the case in the global village (see also the article by Marie-Claire Foblets in this volume).

Romantic love may thus come to be seen as less of a Western value - and as less valued and protected in Western societies - than when Rougemont wrote his book in the thirties. The existence of the notion of romantic love on a global scale seems to challenge the economic rationale behind the establishment of for instance the European Union. Love and love relations that fall under the jurisdiction of EC Law are not protected as a value in themselves, but as requirement for productivity gains.

I do however think that when love or emotions and law meet it will be within the framework of a broader understanding of love than that of romantic love, as it will be in a broader understanding of law than that of positive law.

I think what will meet are discourses of love and justice rather than love and law. They may be related to non-heterosexual relations, to intergenerational relations (a return of the importance of paternal love, the relations between foetus and mother), to inter-national and inter-racial relations, to inter-species relations. And they may concern both individual and collective relations and both emotions that are considered 'destructive' and 'constructive'.

The renewed discourse about natural law, morality and ethics is one expression of a meeting ground of law and emotions, of acknowledging the importance of legal sentiments (Rechtsgefühl).

Maffesoli discusses the relation between ethics and aesthetics and claims that the grounds of condition of collective life in post-modernity is sensitivity, communication and collective emotion, and that the source of energy will be intention or artistic will. The ethical function of aesthetics is according to him to provide common and collective experience. Aesthetic serves as cement, and determines a new form of solidarity in complex societies. It also leads to a collapse of the separation between nature and culture. Nature becomes culturalized and culture becomes naturalized. Maffesoli claims that faculties of sympathy and capacities for action are closely related. The aesthetic dimension might ensure social synergy and bring out the effectiveness of forms of social affinity and sympathy. The culture of postmodernity is a culture of sensation (Gefühlskultur), which moves from a logic of identity to a logic of identification. The thematic of postmodernism is a movement from liberation to attraction or sensuality.

If these observations are correct, as I believe they are, they foresee an important role for cultural normative forms such as film and music in creating - and re-creating - community and communal balance, attraction and harmony. The implications of this for our conception of law could perhaps be that we should look more into a re-creation of a more 'sensual', 'visual', 'musical' and/or rhythmic form of order, if we want also 'law' to contribute to a process of establishing balance and harmony both on a local and global level.

If emotions return - not just in the preambles of conventions and legislations, but more intrinsically in the understandings of 'law', then 'Love, Power and Justice' might perhaps be seen as the unity the theologian Paul Tillich claims they are in his book of this title (1956).

> *'Love is the drive towards the unity of the separated... It is the fulfilment and the triumph of love that it is able to reunite the most radically separated beings, namely individual persons. The individual person is both most separated and the bearer of the most powerful love...' (Tillich p.25 and 26).*

Love is the foundation, not the negation, of power (p.49) and love is also the principle of justice (p.57). Tillich lists four principles and three levels of justice. The four principles are adequacy, equality, personality, and community.

The levels of justice are: justice of everything that has being; tributive or proportional justice (which is the norm within the realm of law and law-enforcement), and transforming of creative justice. This last level or form of justice is based on the fact that intrinsic justice is dynamic.

> *'As in its application to man, so in its application to God justice means more than proportional justice. It means creative justice and is expressed in the divine grace which forgives in order to reunite.' (p.66)*

> *'As in power, justice is immanent in love. A love of any type, and love as a whole if it does not include justice, is chaotic self-surrender, destroying him who loves as well as him who accepts such love. Love is the drive for reunion of the separated. It presupposes that there is something to be reunited, something relatively independent that stands upon itself. Sometimes the love of complete self-surrender has been praised and called the fulfilment of love..*
> *The surrender of such an emaciated self is not genuine love because it extinguishes and does not unite what is estranged. The love of this kind is the desire to annihilate one's responsible and creative self for the sake of the participation in another self which by the assumed act of love is made responsible for himself and oneself. The chaotic self-surrender does not give justice to the other one, because he who surrenders did not give justice to himself. It is justice to oneself to affirm one's own power of being and to accept the claim for justice which is implied in this power. Without this justice there is no reuniting love, because there is nothing to unite...*
> *(pp.68-69).*

> *'Love does not do more than justice demands, but love is the ultimate principle of justice. Love reunites; justice preserves what is to be united. It is the form in which and through which love performs its work. Justice in its ultimate meaning is creative justice, and creative justice is the form of reuniting love'.*
> *(p.71)*

In the claim for a 'just love' Tillich seems to predict contemporary (feminist) fear of romantic love and claims for a more reasonable love.

In this understanding of love as the ultimate principle of justice he seems to echo Kierkegaard's - also Christian - claim of 'love as the fulfilment of law'. I believe we are now in a situation where tributive or proportional justice cannot any longer fulfil the demands for justice in the realm of law and law-enforcement. Also in this realm there is a need for a more nuanced understanding of justice - and perhaps one that comprises consideration of the subjective much more.

Love is seen as a unifying force not just in theology but also in psychology (Lear 1990), which has been considered a 'subjective' science. However Lear declares that if 'love is a basic force in nature, then we must abandon the idea that an external study gives us the way man really is' (Lear 1990, p.182). According to Lear, there is a tendency to believe that any 'internal' validation must be non-objective, and that it is the external perspective that gives us the way things really are.

It is obvious that claims of linking love and justice will be criticized for aiming to link the particular and the general, the subjective and the objective, and thus 'contaminate' the general and objective perspective. However as Magritte has shown in several of his paintings the so-called scientific and objective perspective was also artificial and illusory. We are in a period that is doing away with former opposites such as public and private, objective and subjective, and where the very category of science (if jurisprudence was ever one) is being reevaluated.

I am not suggesting that jurisprudence should become a subjective science to meet love, but that those interested in matters of emotions and normativity, and that lawyers, legal academics, and lay people alike should participate in the general reevaluation of objectiveness and subjectiveness.

Notes:

1 The terms: sites of emotional experience, or emotional sites, are used by Norman K. Denzin in his article 'On understanding Emotion: The interpretive cultural Agenda' (1990).

2 Women's Law in Norway has been using the visual media for purposes of education about formal legality several times during the last decades. The Woman and Law in Southern Africa (WLSA) project has among its actitivites also contributed to the production of a film 'Neria' (produced in Zimbabwe), which deals with the issues of inheritance, and the different legal and other problems it poses to women.In Pakistan NGO's and Female Lawyers associations have also used videos for legal literacy purposes.

3 Examples could be the already mentioned film trilogy by Kieslowski which was if I remember correctly financed by the EU and France, and the film 'Once Were Warriors' about anomia and violence in a Maori community in New Zealand, which if I my information is correct was filmed by Maories themselves.

4 In her small book '*On violence*' Hannah Arendt has some very interesting reflections upon the relation between statehood and violence and law and violence. The sanctions of laws are not their essence she writes, but are directed against those citizens, who - without withholding their support - wish to make an exception for themselves (Arendt 1970, Note 62, p.97).

5 Viroli according to informations in the book is associate professor at the department of politics at Princeton University. In spite of his Italian sounding name, and many Italian examples in the book, it seems to have been written in English in the first place and is dedicated to Norberto Bobbio.

References:

Anderson, Benedict (1985): *Imagined Communities. Reflections on the Origin and Spread of Nationalism.* Verso, Norfolk.

Arendt, Hannah (1970): *On Violence.* Harcourt Brace & Company, San Diego, New York, London.

Blackmur, R.P. (1956): *The Lion and the Honeycomb. Essays in Solicitude and Critique.* Methuen and Co.Ltd. London.

Denzin, Norman K. (1990): 'On understanding Emotion: The Interpretive-Cultural Agenda'. In Theodore D. Kemper (ed.): *Research Agendas in the Sociology of Emotions.* State University of New York Press. pp.85-116.

Honoré, Anne Marie (1994): *Filmpolitik midt i en medierevolution.* [Film politics in the middle of a media revolution] Nordisk Kultur Institut. Klim, Denmark.

Johansen, Martin (1994): *Følelser. Lidt om nogen af dem* (Emotions. A little bit about some of them). Nyt Nordisk Forlag. Arnold Busck.

Koselleck, R. (1981): Die Auflösung des Hauses als ständischer Herrschaftseinheit. In Bulst et al (Hrsgb): *Familie zwischen Tradition und Moderne.* Vandenhoeck & Ruprecht. Göttingen.

Langer, Susanne K. (1969): *Menneske og Symbol. En studie i fornuftens, ritualets og kunstens symboler.* (Man and Symbol). Gyldendal.

Lear, Jonathan (1990): *Love and its Place in Nature. A Philosophical Interpretation of Freudian Psychoanalysis.* Faber and Faber, London.

Lindhardt, Jan (1993): *Frem mod middelalderen. TV - det levende billede i det åbne rum.* [Towards the Middle Ages. TV - the living image in the open space]. GAD, Copenhagen.

Maeckelberghe, Els Lisette Maria (1991): *Desperately Seeking Mary. A Feminist Appropriation of a Traditional Religious Symbol.* Rijksuniversiteit Groningen.

Maffesoli, Michael (1991): 'The Ethic of Aesthetics'. In *Theory, Culture & Society,* Vol 8. pp. 7-20.

McClary, Susan: *Feminine Endings. Music, Gender and Sexuality* (1991).

Nousiainen, Kevät (1993): 'Juridiskt språk och nationalitet' (Legal Language and Nationality). In Retfærd, no. 63, pp.60-72.

Paz, Octavio (1988): *Sor Juana. Or the Traps of Faith.* The Belknap Press of Harvard University Press, Cambridge, Massachussetts.

Petersen, Hanne (1996): 'Informal norms and gendered labour law' in Kravaritou, Yota (ed.): *The Sex of Labour Law.* Kluwer Law International.

Petersen, Hanne (1996): 'Famiglie di donne e famiglie giuridice. Le esperienze dei paesi nordici'. In Guido Maggioni (ed.): *Come Il Diritto Tratta Le Famiglie.* Università degli Studi di Urbino, Istituto de Sociologia, QuattroVenti, 1996, pp.153-181.

Petersen, Hanne (forthcoming): 'The Lion King and the Lady and the Unicorn. Jurisprudential Considerations on Visual Normativity'. Paper for the 17th IVR World Congress in Bologna, to be published in *European Yearbook in the Sociology of Law.*

de Rougemont, Denis (1983): *Love in the Western World.* Revised and augmented edition including new postscript. Princeton University Press. Princeton, New Jersey.

Tillich, Paul (1954): *Love, Power and Justice. Ontological Analyses and Ethical Applications.* Oxford University Press.

Viroli, Maurizio (1995): *For Love of Country. An Essay on Patriotism and Nationalism.* Clarendon Press, Oxford.

On Love and other Injustices. Love and law as improbable communications

KOEN RAES

Let me not to the marriage of true minds
Admit impediments. Love is not love
Which alters when it alteration finds,
Or bends with the remover to remove;
O, no! it is an ever-fixed mark,
That looks on tempests and is never shaken;
It is the star to every wandering bark,
Whose worth's unknown, although his height be taken
Love's not Time's fool, though rosy lips and cheeks
Within his bending sickle's compass come;
Love alters not with his brief hours and weeks,
But bears it out even to the edge of doom.
If this be error and upon me proved,
I never writ, nor no man ever loved.
W. Shakespeare, Sonnet 116

1. Love's discourse

Writing *about* love, as something external to the game of language, as an object of inquiry that may be observed, analyzed and valued by means of words and sentences which do not themselves express love, raises some puzzling difficulties. First, love is part of a culturally embedded 'practice', in the sense MacIntyre defined it, and appears, on that behalf, to be understandable only as an 'internal good'; one cannot 'know' what love 'is' unless one understands the 'practice of loving' within western culture and perhaps one cannot know what love 'is' until one loves and is loved. Second, love presents itself as covering the domain of the unspoken, as being beyond speech, as an emotion that cannot be uttered or expressed by words. Language can only be a poor expression of what love really is.

According to Foucault, the launching and circulation of particular discourses on certain issues that were for a long period almost taboo, should not be taken as a sign of greater openness and understanding (Foucault, 1976). On the contrary, they may be tools to restrict and to 'normalize' what formerly remained unproblematic. The 'will to know' and the resulting free flow of information are not, by definition, liberating forces. Thus, *'la mise en discours du sexe'* became, during the 19th century, the very tool to discipline, and to control the 'sexual appetite' and to reduce eroticism as an *ars erotica* to sexuality as a *scientia sexualis*. Could it, in a similar vein, be argued that *'la mise en discours de l'amour'* is only a way to shape it within normative boundaries? Is increasing talk *about* love rather a sign that love becomes the object of normalizing forces than an expression of its liberation? Shouldn't love be recognized as being beyond speech and belonging to the mystical domain Wittgenstein referred to in his conclusion to the Tractatus : *'Worüber Man nicht sprechen kann, darüber muss Man schweigen'?*

Apparently not. The relation between love and language is not simply comparable to the relation between sexuality and language. Talk about love did not as easily as talk about sexuality give rise to a 'scientification' of its subject, although it should be admitted that in the modern era, love is often approached from within a 'therapeutic perspective', as being a 'means' toward happiness, satisfaction and 'the good life' and thus becomes part of the cult of privatism with obvious political implications (Lasch, 1977).

But the relation between love and language is in the main not so instrumental and extrinsic. On the contrary, it could be argued that love only exists in and through language, that it was by means of speech acts - the songs of the troubadours, lyric poetry and love letters - that love was created, as a cultural artefact, so to say. *'Il y a des gens qui n'auraient jamais été amoureux s'ils n'avaient entendu parler de l'amour'* wrote La Rochefoucauld in the 18th century. And indeed, it is hardly possible to overlook the influence of books such as *La Nouvelle Héloise* by Jean Jacques Rousseau or *Die Leiden des jungen Werthers* by Johann Wolfgang Goethe on the dissemination of the romantic love figure in 19th century Western culture and which made modern love so radically different from the seductive games described in Chloderlos de Laclos' *Les liaisons dangereuses*.

Language is not extrinsic to love. Love does not exist independent from any written or speech act. Rather than being difficult to grasp in language, it is created and recreated by it. Love longs for language for its confirmation. Language arouses love. For the language of love, it may indeed be true that *'il n'y a pas de hors texte'*. The 'unspoken' mystery of love is not opposed to speech. It is permanently suggested, fostered and excited by it. In language, love longs for incessant confirmation of its existence. Language may be expressive both of the longing for a beloved one and of the longing for love itself. Language may provoke love for the sake of love.

2. Law's negation

If the culture of western love is integrally related to the culture of the written word, this could be interpreted as a point wherein love resembles law. For law too is intrinsically discursive, requires language for its foundation, validation and operation.

Yet, even if love shares its 'discursivity' with law, its language game is structured in radical opposition to legal discourse. Whilst love was, for a long time, an external challenge to the legally structured marital bond, existing independent from it and not aiming at replacing it, it became in modern times the very foundation of marriage, without thereby losing its nature of contradicting all of legality's presuppositions.

In the history of western ideas, the dominant script about love and loving relationships depicts them as the very negation of the ideas of law and legality. In love persons meet one another in their wholeness and total complexity, whilst any legal relationship is characterized by more or less traceable boundaries and identities. Love is radically personal and particularistic; there is no such thing as universal love (the humanist proclaiming his love for 'humankind' therewith proves never to have known love at all, wrote Sartre in *La nausée*). Law aims at generality, without making distinctions based on personal traits of character. Law facilitates social bonds between strangers or 'unencumbered selves'. Love is an intimate bond between significant others. The intrinsic spontaneity and emotionality of the loving affection contradicts the idea of rule governed behaviour that is fundamental for law. Love implies involvement, law requires detachment, love implies partiality (*is* partiality), law requires impartiality. According to authors such as Aubert (1967), Unger (1976) or Luhmann (1982) - is it a mere accident that so many sociologists of law (including Marx) took an interest in love as 'the very negation of law'? - love is all that law cannot and may not be. Love is spontaneity and uncertainty, it is unreasonable and unpredictable. Love is unconventional, unjust and challenges all of morality. Legal relations are calculative and cool, love relationships are irresponsible and hot. Love is described as a mental illness ('une folie à deux'), aroused by a poison and enslaving the subject. Love is unlawfulness.

Ever since Hume introduced the radical distinction between reason and desire, declared reason itself devoid of content and saw desire as a mere bundle of appetites without any consistency or rationality, no satisfying relation between both could be established (Unger, 1975). The struggle between 'reason' and 'desire' developed into one of the major subjects of ethical theorizing with on the one hand philosophers such as Kant, taking sides with pure, formal reason from which all moral rules should be derived if moral obligation is to be autonomous (deriving morality from desire would result in a heteronomous morality) and, on the other hand, philosophers such as Bentham, who agreed that no substantial morality could be derived from desire, but argued that the maximization of pleasure could be used as a normative, instrumental yardstick to found moral rules. Reason became thus either part of a non-natural realm or the (instrumental) slave of our passions. Reasonable desires are a contradictio in terminis; the relation between reason and desire is either a relation of domination, when reason disciplines the passions, or a relation of maximization, when reason is dedicated to developing the most efficient means to realize a non-reasonable goal. In both, reason and desire are extrinsic to one another. This great divide still dominates western moral thinking and, more generally, western culture as a whole for the struggle between reason and desire became one of the central themes in modern art production.

Law, belonging to the realm of ('public') reason, privatized desire and with it the object of masculine desire, the woman (Elshtain, 1981; Pateman, 1988). Love became obsessive possession by men, unconditional surrender by women and both sentiments were extra-legal. Love could not be considered an element of legal relations. But it became, nevertheless, the motivating force underneath one of law's and society's most important institutions: marriage. Love was recognized as the non-legal foundation of legal obligation.

3. The manifold sources of western love

The culture of western love has its roots in a variety of traditions. One of these traditions is *religious* and evolved from the christian faith in an outer-wordly realm of true alliance, as the very negation of the inner-wordly vale of tears. The more christianity worshipped a *contemptus mundo, vitae et homini*, the more it could foster the longing for a kingdom of eternal grace, guaranteed by god, the very negation of all earthly worries. Religious faith required absolute surrender and exclusiveness, and so does love (Ortega Y Gasset, 1969). The *tremendum and fascinans* emanating from the sacred is also present in love's contemplation of the beloved one, whilst the loving union in the orgasm can be compared to religious ecstacy, as a feeling which transcends finite beings. Making loving is making the supreme sacrifice. Both love and religion aim at immortality, at the confirmation of life beyond death. (Bataille, 1957) Monotheism and monogamy seem to be interrelated: 'one god, one lover'. There are strong affinities between the meaning of religious 'faith' and what is implied in the 'faithfulness' of lovers. Not accidentally, the catholic church saw in the loving relationship between mortals a strong rival, so as to prohibit the clergy to be involved in 'earthly love'. Priests and nuns should only worship one god and in order to spread the universal religion, priests are not allowed to entertain particularistic relationships. As Plato's guardians, their cause should be the *civitas dei*, not the *communitas amori*.

A second tradition is *religious* also, but has, according to De Rougemont (1956), its roots rather in oriental religion, in the cult of *eros*, rather than *agape*. Here, faith becomes a real passion and aims at mystic union - often with explicit erotic undertones - with the divine. The mystic culture of love is a culture of the longing for an orgastic elevation to the purest form of community with god. The 'élan suprême' of mystic love aspires to an 'uplifting' from the earth, a 'dépassement infini', the ascension of man to god, which is a point of no return. In a way, love is here the longing for the 'Aufhebung' of any wordly limitation, for dissolution into something or someone else.

Another tradition is the culture of *courtship* and *chivalry* with its games of 'dating' and 'mating', its playfulness and gallantry, yet also its pathos and sincerity. The culture of courtship was profoundly erotic and directed to bodily satisfaction. Simultaneously however, it somehow entertained already the message which Kierkegaard elaborated in his *Journal of a young seducer*, that desire could be more intense than satisfaction, either as the ex ante desire of a lover awaiting his beloved one or as the ex post desire of a lover remembering a passionate night.

The fourth tradition is *Dyonisian* and has been firmly opposed by the church who rather stood for the Appolonian tradition (Paglia, 1990). In more recent times this tradition developed into the culture of *expressive individualism*, as it arose from the romantic era. Romantic love stands in the sign of authenticity, the purely human ('rein menschliche') 'union' of two souls and bodies, sharing a common we-identity which is in total harmony with 'nature'. Love is here an aspect of the self-realization of a person through another person, an expression of true emotions, sincere feelings and real humanity which is opposed to 'society', with its alienating codes and roles. Love is not only a feeling, but also a desire for reciprocal bodily satisfaction; it is sensitive and sensual, erotic and sexual, natural and spontaneous.

Although these traditions have in common that they all imply lovers to take some distance from society (its rules, conventions, its public sphere and norms) and to experience love in some secret space, as an 'égoisme à deux', and although they have in common a total neglect of procreative solicitudes (although this biological consequence of 'loving' was always present as a somewhat alien danger) thereby clearly illustrating a gendered bias in favour of a male approach to love, their combination could not but result in contradictions; between the longing for eternity and the longing for sexual gratification, between playing according to particular codes and expressing one's true feelings, between expressiveness and faithfullness etc. Modern love, that is, is in itself already a bundle of tensions and contradictions. Confronted with law they result in contradictory forms of life. Western love aims at combining unreconcilable aspirations and the western culture of love is indeed nothing else but the never ending story of the confrontation of love's manifold desires.

Love's esthetical caprices cannot but irritate the seriousness of love's ethical commitments whilst love's longing for bodily - and thus finite - union stands in the way of love's religious quest for eternal salvation.

Kierkegaard tried to integrate some of love's directions, by putting them into succesive stages. He exalts passionate love as the supreme value in the esthetical stage of life, argues that this love exceeds itself in marriage as the supreme value of the ethical stage of life and finally condemns marriage as a major obstacle to the religious stage, because it binds us to innerwordly temporality whilst true love seeks eternity. (Kierkegaard, 1943) Most people, however, do not live such ordered (?) lives and are rather involved in a incessant quest for the simultaneous satisfaction of all of love's promises.

4. Marriage as love's ethics?

Whilst the legitimacy of eternal commitments was radically questioned in the legal conception of personhood and obligation as they resembled slavery, only in love such an eternal bond - or at least the longing for such a bond - could persist as it reflects the very essence of the loving effect. Persons may love different persons at different moments of time so that it seems as if love is only a temporary engagement, limited in duration. But any loving relationship contains and is built upon the promise of eternity and is as such legally enacted ('till death parts us'). It would be contrary to the understanding of love to put in advance a term on the relationship and no empirical knowledge about the factual temporary nature of love relationships and the resulting 'polygamy over time' is able to change this fundamental attitude.

This infinitude of love has puzzled western legal systems ever since they institutionalized marriage on the basis of it. How could law arise from and structure loving relationships, whilst remaining faithful to its liberal and consensual foundations, rejecting the legitimacy of eternal engagements ? How could law compel people to faithfulness whilst the eventual moral value of faith is exactly founded on its spontaneous fulfilment? How could law, furthermore, prohibit, yes even persecute, certain loving relationships, whilst it proclaimed love to be the essential foundation of marriage? If love and free will are recognized as what makes human relations legitimate, how can this very same love and the very same free will create something illegitimate? Legal systems can hardly develop consistent regulations to grasp all of the complexities of a loving affection, considered to be both essential to and destabilizing its fundamental institutions.

William Godwin was one of the first to reveal the contradiction between modern liberal individualism and the institution of marriage. In his *Enquiry concerning political obligation* (1793), he rejected everything understood by the term cooperation as 'in some sense an evil'. For, so he argued, *'it is absurd to expect the inclinations and wishes of two human beings to coincide, through any long period of time'.* (Godwin, 1979, 761) Marriage between loving partners could only institutionalize the impossible: *'To oblige them to act and to live together is to subject them to some inevitable portion of thwarting, bickering and unhappiness. This cannot be otherwise, so long as men shall continue to vary in their habits, their preferences and their views. No man is always cheerful and kind; and it is better that his fits of irritation should subside of themselves, since the mischief in that case is more limited, and since the jarring of opposite tempers, and the suggestion of a wounded pride, tend inexpressibly to increase the irritation'.* (Godwin, 1979, 761- 762) Marriage is an evil and the western culture of marriage only survives by making use of tricks:

'The method is for a thoughtless and romantic youth of each sex to come together, to see each other, for a few times and under circumstances full of delusion, and then to vow eternal attachment...In almost every instance they find themselves deceived. They are reduced to make the best of an irretrievable mistake. They are led to conceive it their wisest policy to shut their eyes upon realities, happy, if by any perversion of intellect, they can persuade themselves that they were right in their first crude opinion of each other. Thus the institution of marriage is made a system of fraud; and men who carefully mislead their judgments in the daily affair of their life must be expected to have a crippled judgment in every other concern'. (Godwin, 1979, 762)

More generally, it was the view of Godwin that *'We ought to be able to do without one another. He is the most perfect man to whom society is not a necessity of life, but a luxury, innocent and enviable, in which he joyfully indulges. Such a man will not fly to society, as to something requisite for the consuming of his time, or the refuge of his weakness. In society he will find pleasure; the temper of his mind will prepare him for friendship and for love. But he will resort with a scarcely inferior eagerness to solitude; and he will find in it the highest complacency and the purest delight'.* (Godwin, 1979, 761)

Godwin's personal life story perhaps illustrates more than anything else the 'impossible realism' of this kind of liberal individualism which celebrates freely chosen (time for) loving relationships. His partner, Mary Wollstonecraft, got pregnant and both felt the 'communitarian' pressure to marry after all. Mary died in childbirth, giving birth to Mary Wollstonecraft Shelley, the later author of Frankenstein. The chosen commitments of William and Mary were not able to handle the unwilled and neither could they simply get rid of what they had not chosen expressis verbis. This has been the fate of thousands of lovers until recent times. And even today, in this age of contraception and birth control, unchosen commitments often arise within relationships that were explicitly established to avoid them. The will may control childbirth in a negative direction, but many couples find it difficult to accept that willing is not enough to pursue parenthood. (Lauritzen, 1993) Similarly, one may will 'a' child but at least until now, one cannot will 'this' particular child; parenthood inevitably involves unchosen commitments. This is true for the loving bond between partners as well, for however much one anticipates - through contracts - all that could happen, it is simply impossible to fix the future. Love has more to do with fate than the modern point of view is prepared to accept.

Godwin's sound judgment that it is quite improbable that two people find in their relation satisfaction in all dimensions of their (multiple) being, remains pertinent and is echoed in Leo Tolstoy's bitter condemnation of marriage and its so-called domestic peace as nothing but hell on earth. Even more, taking into account rising expectations of post-war European youngsters concerning their future partners, durable unions seem all the more unlikely. (Elchardus & Heyvaert, 1990) If one and the same person should incarnate the values of intelligence, spontaneity, responsibility, carefulness, sensuality, faithfulness, tenderness, courageousness, thriftiness, cordiality, playfulness and sincerity it is hardly surprising that many partners are easily disappointed in one another. Partners can either adapt their preferences to more realistic expectations, resign to a sub-optimal relationship, get involved in several relationships or leave it in view of finding eventually a more fitting companion.

It could be expected that in the era of expressive individualism, more and more people would become aware of the reduction of the gains to institutionalize their loving bond in the legal form of a marital contract. But this is only partly true. What is more, in all western countries unmarried couples as well as homosexual relations claim legal recognition as a permanent engagement, in the name of an affection, law itself proclaimed to be foundational for marriage. In Europe, this struggle for an equal treatment and an equal recognition of non-heterosexual love (including equal inheritance, adoption and custody-rights) has now come to the point of opening marriage - or something very much resembling it - to homosexuals. Many oppose such an evolution and argue that this would mean the very 'end of marriage'. However, such an evolution is consistently in line with founding marriage on love and free will.

If love and free will are the only legitimate grounds to enter a marital bound, there is no reason whatsoever to bar non-heterosexual relations out of it. On the contrary, a non-loving or non-free heterosexual relationship stands much more in contradiction to the modern figure of marriage than a loving and free homosexual one. If lovers have the right to ignore social status or cultural and national boundaries, why shouldn't the law be neutral as far as sexual preferences are concerned as well?

In a similar perspective, conservatives argued for a long time that divorce contradicts the institution of marriage. But here again, divorce is the natural consequence of founding marriage *both* on love and free will.

It is true that those who give a religious meaning to the marital bond accept that 'holy matrimony' is not a mere intersubjective contract. According to the catholic creed, marriages are made in heaven and are, in this sense, initiated by god. And what is initiated by god cannot be dissolved by a human decision ('what god hath joined together, let not man put asunder'). But even within the catholic conception of marriage as an indissoluble union, it is accepted that if there was no 'true' love when partners entered marriage, no marriage ever existed.

What could be exactly the meaning of 'choosing', for the whole of one's life, a partner? Common sense moralists may well recommend that partners should carefully reflect before taking a decision, as if the choice of a partner depends on a well-defined number of reasons and as if persons have some fixed identity and some fixed relationship with one another. But no one is able to predict one's and one's partner's future self. One cannot 'fix the future'. Strangely enough, exactly this uncertainty is often invoked as a *reason* to marry, as a reason to 'legalize' one's engagement; marriage as a way to 'bind oneself' under circumstances when perhaps love has faded way. Marriage as a contract against one's future selves, one's future love.

The ethics of marriage requires that lovers should calculate their chances of finding happiness in founding a household on their shared love. But the contractual language of law cannot conceal that the promise of marriage is rather taking a chance and this stands at right angles to the irrevocability of the marital vow. The quest for eternity may well be a sincere feeling, but that does not yet make it a relevant legal category. The only guarantee for the truthfulness of lovers lies in the sincerity of their intentions, not in the legal rules concerning marriage they are prepared to accept. This sincerity is only reflected but not expressed in legal rules, in the sense that true lovers would be prepared to promise *anything* to one another, if this would be required to prove their love. As far as these intentions are concerned, there is, in this sense, no difference between the promise 'to die' or 'to go to prison' as a proof of one's sincere feelings for a beloved one and the promise to stay together for life, whatever may happen. As Denis de Rougemont argues, not the promise of fidelity is problematic, but what exactly follows from it. *'Ce n'est pas l'engagement qui est problématique, mais les conséquences qu'il entraine'*. (De Rougemont, 1956, 258) Fidelity has no reasons and neither is infidelity a proof that one's promise to be faithful was insincere. Love's exclusiveness cannot be translated into something like an exclusive contract of concession. Infidelity is not simply a breach of contract giving rise to the payment of damages. The way law views and treats infidelity or a divorce is not similar to the way partners experience their infidelity or their separation. The legal doctrine of hidden faults is hardly applicable in the domain of marriage settlements (although the popular saying that *'en marriage, il trompe qui peut'* reflects rather a premodern conception of marriage, even the modern approach has never extended the doctrine of contract so as to embrace the whole of the marital engagement) and anyway, the motives why partners stay together or separate are not easily reflected in the 'reasons' the law recognizes as legitimate grounds.

Whilst the promise of fidelity may be sincere, to enforce it by law is morally contradictory. What could be the value of an enforced faithfulness? What would partners think of each other if they knew that the only reason for the faithfulness of their husband or wife is that the law obliges them to do so?

Marriage has never been a mere 'contract'; it is an institution. Partners have almost no say in the terms of the contract and cannot simply bargain about their rights and obligations. Opting for marriage is opting to *enter* a social institution, not to close a contract. For the same reason partners cannot on their own decide to dissolve the contract; this is the judge's competence. In a way, this still reflects the religious foundation of marriage as a sacrament with a dimension which transcends the competence of the partners involved.

But even as an institution, the legitimacy of marriage relies upon love, and upon nothing else. If love, as an intersubjective bond, is accepted as the foundation of marriage, it should be accepted as well that if there is no more love, there is no more reason to remain in a marital state. Forcing people to remain married would either mean to force them to love one another - and this is exactly what the modern script on love does not accept - or to force them to stay married whilst not loving one another, and this could mean that intra-marital rape would be permitted. This is radically opposed to the right to physical integrity of both spouses; even as a 'union' they remain separate individuals, with borders the other cannot trespass without his/her consent. Love may be infinite in its intentions, but no legal consequences can be derived from it. Infinitude or eternity have no legal implications. Love is all that is required to marry and although the 'sense of eternity' may be part of the loving affection, it is no part of its legal dimension. When love fades away, this is legal reason enough to opt out of the institution of marriage.

Love and human rights have nevertheless transformed marriage in a fundamental way. For whilst marriage is indeed an institution aiming at, amongst other things, the regulation of sexuality, it cannot install claim rights in this field as it can install claim rights to support or alimony. There is no such thing as a 'claim-right to sexual intercourse' within marriage as an individual right. The right to sexual intercourse is within or outside marriage nothing but a licence - right: it is permitted, but cannot be requested by the partner. It only exists as a 'shared right', as a right 'between consenting adults'. But no partner may be forced to sexual intercourse against his or her will. Even within marriage this is now considered as rape and thus punishable. The legal implications of this are rather surprising. For if both partners have the right to say 'no', they may claim this right not only at one particular moment, they may claim it as long as pleases them. Now if we accept at the same time that sexual intercourse is a human right as well, we should conclude that a partner, confronted with the 'no' of his wife or her husband, must derive from the mere fact that the partner refuses sexual intercourse either (a) *a right to commit adultery* or (b) *a right to divorce*. The recognition of human rights within marriage has thus contributed to the erosion of marriage as an institution.

It seems that love dominates motives and the beginning of affective interhuman relationships, whilst law dominates their dissolution. This should come as no surprise. Whilst a detached, matter of fact approach is of no use when affections urge people positively to one another, to shared experiences, it is all the more required when affections drive people away from each other and when questions of distribution and dissolution take precedence. Love melts together, law divides. Love is 'the art of fusion', law is 'the art of separation'.

Modern marriage contained the promise to combine affective and reasonable communication, by allowing love to be the founding motive of marriage, whilst law structured its implications and consequences. But in fact they are thus related to one another in a complementary way and not an integral way; love pushes legality in the background and law only appears, when love fades away.

5. Adulterous love against marriage

The modern interrelatedness of love and marriage has thus not solved their opposing tendencies. The tension between law and love has a long history. Western culture inherited it from the romantic era, spiced by religious as well as courtly ingredients, which lay the foundations of the sentimental, bourgeois family (Okin, 1981) but it already has strong roots, as Denis de Rougemont argued, in the troubadour culture of the middle ages. Sentimental love as the basic motivation to engage in marriage became one of the most democratized institutions in western society, embracing all classes. Although it was for a long time characterized by patriarchal domination and by the privatization of women's lives, it could develop into the very soil for (a not yet wholly realized) equality and equal respect between the sexes (Badinter, 1986). Yet this very same sentimental love developed into the most undermining force of marriage; when love fades away, no reason exists any more to stay together. When love changes direction, the institution of marriage should follow its course. It is no accident that the problem of marital faith and the ever present possibility of passionate seduction is an everlasting subject in the modern novel. The fact of no more being a desired person after marriage seems to be an unattractive perspective. Marriage thus has to remain a challenged bond, faith should always be prepared to stand the test of new adventures. The promise of emotional rest should always be put to the test as long as love is at issue. Any loving bond contains the promise of an even more appealing one. From Flaubert's *Madame Bovary*, Stendal's *Le rouge et le noir*, Tolstoy's *Anna Karenina*, Fontana's *Effi Briest*, Scott Fitzgerald's *The great Gatsby* until Lawrence's *Lady Chatterley's lover* a struggle is going on between romantic or passionate love and marriage, a struggle which is typically understood in terms of a struggle between human nature and social conventions, between desire and reason, between spontaneity and morality. A superficial look at popular literature or television soap shows how very well this struggle is recognized by the public. Perhaps no culture has invested so much of its artistic talents in unravelling love's wanderings. Perhaps no culture is so obsessed with love's promise and marriage's failure than western culture. It is curious that people seem never to have enough of the story of love's caprices and intrigues and it seems that in the imaginary world of literature and film - not to mention pop-music - people search for all that remained unfulfilled in their own love story.

Curiously enough, the paradigmatic love affair in (admittedly, male-dominated) western literature is, ever since *Tristan and Isolde*, adulterous love, and not the love between unmarried youngsters. And in most cases, the tragedy of love is about women who are invited or seduced to commit adultery. This cannot be accidental; there must be some deeply felt point of recognition in the cult of Tristan and Isolde, Werther and Lotte, Anna Karenina and Wronsky, Jay and Daisy or Constance Chatterley and Mellors. It is the unbound male who challenges the marital fidelity of the female. Masculine adultery does not raise such dramatic choices as feminine adultery, perhaps because it is much more expected from men than from women; Don Juan is the archetype of the male lover, a lover without commitments, adored but at the same time abhorred by (married) women for the emotions he may release in them. For women, this is a true challenge, a dangerous threat; they have no way to entertain both a husband and a lover. These women are imprisoned by an unhappy marriage and an unbounded lover invites them to throw away the chains. This really threatens the 'foundations' of society, the foundations of morality. It is as if the prohibition of adultery makes adulterous love so compelling, as if, in the words of Bataille (1957), the prohibition exists in order to be violated. This cannot but result in drama. Yet the drama is very human and whilst the male lovers in these stories are as much in love with the woman as with their love itself, female lovers are confronted with the social and moral consequences of giving way to their most profound feelings. They thus become fallen women, heroines without a future.

Love contains the promise of marriage. But marriage always implies the promise of something else, something beyond marriage, something preceding marriage, something opposing marriage whilst at the same time leading to a new promise of hapiness within a new marriage. Marriage thus appears both to negate love and at the same time to remain the natural result of a loving bond for the promise of marriage celebrates the truthfulness of the loving sentiment.

Modern love, it should be emphasized, is intrinsically though in contradictory ways related to the underlying, liberal figure of free choice. Whatever the truth might have been of Samuel Johnson's dictum *'Marriages would in general be as happy, and often more so, if they were all made by the Lord Chancellor'*, it is so alien to our understanding of marriage not to leave the decision to the partners involved, that arranged marriages would simply not function anymore (although, it should be admitted, Moon has many followers in the western world as well and although more and more marriage brokers are engaged in the search for an ideal partner, our impersonal public culture does not allow for many spontaneous encounters between strangers)

However, the interrelations between freedom and love are complicated and contradictory. Freedom refers to 'choice', to the realm of the will. But love escapes the will, belongs to another world than the world of choice, promises and contract. Love cannot, as Elster argued, be willed, one cannot 'will' to fall (!) in love.(Elster, 1986) Perhaps the will can resist love, but it cannot create love. In numerous operas, such as Bizet's *Carmen*, Puccini's La *Bohème* and *Madame Butterfly* or Verdi's *La Traviata* the will is presented as powerless when confronted with love (and, interestingly, it is mostly the woman who becomes the final victim of the loving effect). Love is exalted in western culture but ever since the legend of *Tristan and Isolde* or of *Romeo and Juliet*, the fate of love ends in poison and tragedy as if our culture expresses the belief that love, or at least the happiness that is promised by love is not of this world, has to transcend worldly conditions and institutions. The promises of love result in death and although lovers know their fate to be suffering and despair, nothing can stop them. Desire is stronger than happiness, destroys happiness.

6. Subversive love?

Love directs the will, yet is said to be blind. Reason is 'the slave of our passions' but nevertheless, the so-called freedom of choice of partners is exalted. There is no relation whatsoever between the 'willingness to pay' which is said to dominate market relations and the 'willingness to love' which dominates relationships. Consequently, any attempt to reduce marriage to a chain of interpersonal contracts fails. No law can embrace all that people 'mean' when they decide to marry.

Exactly the unconventional nature of passionate, romantic love has inspired many critical thinkers of the modern era - such as Charles Fourier, Wilhelm Reich or Reimut Reiche - to look in love for the radically subversive power that would take sides with the oppressed in the anticapitalist struggle for a better world. The good that is incorporated in the loving affection contradicts any conception of the right and the just that is embedded in reigning legal institutions. The non-legal topos is a topos of loving relationships, beyond contract or justice.

However, the subversive power of love can be questioned from an emancipatory point of view.

First, no one can disregard the strong interrelations between possessive individualism and the understanding of love in western culture. But is possessive love and all the manipulative tricks it has at its disposal and as they were analysed in Sartre's *L'être et le néant* (1944) intrinsically liberating?

In 1949, Simone de Beauvoir still could, in *Le Deuxième sexe*, cite approvingly Nietzsche who wrote in *The gay science* that love signifies two different things for man and woman; what women understand by love is not only devotion, but a total gift of body and soul, without reservation, without regard for anything whatever. This makes their love into a faith. If a man loves a woman, he wants exactly that love from her, but he is far from postulating the same sentiment for himself as for the woman. If a man would also feel that desire for complete abandonment, he would, according to Nietzsche, not be a man. (De Beauvoir, 1949, 376)

Should one simply put aside the masculinist and sexist connotations that are deeply embedded in the modern figure of love? One should, at least, take account of Andrea Dworkin's (1987) and Catharine MacKinnon's (1987) impressive deconstruction of western love as an affection dominated by the male's quest for submission, penetration and possession of the female. The language of western love is profoundly imbued with the metaphors of domination and war, not of liberation and peace.

Second, the western notion of love is linked in many ways to a consumerist ideology and its unending quest for always new stimuli and always new sources of satisfaction. The notion of romantic love could easily evolve toward a consumerist conception of love as a passion aiming only at individual gratification. In an age of 'expressive individualism' (Bellah, 1986) love, relationships and marriage are overdetermined by a therapeutic stop which understands affections and relations merely in functionalist terms, in terms of the individual gratifications they can bring about. Our culture is obsessed with an illusion of eternity, creating dissatisfaction and frustration. The sentimentalization of love resulted in its commercializing and 'marketing' and thus rather enforces than criticizes dominant ideology.

Third, the dominant script about love depicts it as a radically anti-social affection; lovers turn their back to society, search for isolation, privacy, intimacy. Love is a private, not a public affair and lovers have the urging right to withdraw from societal troubles. The caring and sharing of lovers is radically particularistic, yes, even egoistic. Subversive this may certainly be but it is not altogether clear in what sense this may lead to societal emancipation.

Finally, it should be admitted that for a long time in our culture, and in the name of love, many practices were covered by 'love' and its privacy that can hardly count as emancipatory. In fact it was often necessary to break the myth of love in order to discover child abuse, rape and women battering. The privacy of love often covers more and other things than what love suggests. The loving bond is not always a 'haven in a heartless world' but could be invoked as an alibi to keep reason and justice out of a relationship.

This is not meant to 'discredit' the loving affect - whatever that could mean. It is rather meant to give law somewhat more credit than it is given in the dominant script, for often, legal regulations created possibilities for a more responsible, more respectful, more egalitarian love. It was often by means of legal communication that loving communications could become somewhat more reasonable. It has no doubt that severing the criminal laws concerning rape, introducing penal laws prohibiting 'uninvited intimacies' and enforcing equality between maried people all have contributed to the emancipation of women, in the public sphere as well as in the private sphere of the household.

This argument is somewhat similar to the argument against those feminists who contrast, as much as possible, an 'ethics of caring' - said to be intrinsically feminine - to an 'ethics of justice' - said to be intrinsically masculine (Noddings, 1984). Whilst there is no doubt that both perspectives give different meanings to 'the moral point of view', it is true as well that, as Badinter argued, greater equality (and freedom) between the sexes was a necessary prerequisite for the caring affection to flourish, not as a mere 'defence of the weak' but as an intrinsically valuable perspective. (Badinter, 1986) A post-conventional 'ethics of caring' does not negate an ethics of justice, but requires such an ethics as a precondition.

So, some notion of justice may be part of the modern idea of love. But it would be a mistake to think that love and justice became allies. What justice is there in choosing the one above the other, when two persons are equally in love with you? What justice is there in persons never finding someone to love or someone loving them? What justice is there in loving relationships evolving, for the greatest part, within a monocultural background? What justice is there in men, mostly falling in love with women younger than themselves and thus creating the problem of loneliness for so many elderly widows? As women live longer than men, it would be a matter of life-span justice if men would mostly fall in love with older women and women with younger men. But is it simply conceivable to enforce such a more just relational distribution?

There is, furthermore, nothing just in the natural lottery which 'distributes' so arbitrarily natural beauty, and there is nothing just in the fact that such 'natural talents' do play their part in the allocation of partners. There is nothing just in the fact that interhuman encounters are to a great extent just a question of luck and that people who really could have loved one another will never meet.

It is seldom justice which will hold back a husband or a wife to fall in love with someone else, even though they have meant and done so much for one another. It is not fair or just that love is blind and irresponsible.

But does it really make sense at all to look at love in terms of justice, or to condemn an 'unjust love'? For even such love remains of value, remains a value of its own, that will resist its condemnation in terms of values that are external to love itself.

7. The future of postmodern love and marriage

It is not altogether clear which way love and marriage will go in the future. Modern culture developed both the technological and ideological conditions to disentangle love, procreation, parenthood, marriage and sex. The legal institution of marriage, though it remained institutionally almost the same, transformed more and more from a patriarchal institution into an egalitarian partnership and, finally became a child-oriented institution.

It seems that at the end of the twentieth century, children are the true building stones of the institution of marriage and that law and society are mainly interested in their fate. In an age where priceless children have become very scarce, their fate is an issue of public concern. (Zelizer, 1981) The main reason to recognize a partnership as an institution is because of the (rights of the) children. All other motives can very well survive without marriage. The postmodern marriage is no more the premodern 'marriage de raison' nor the modern 'marriage des sentiments' than it is a 'marriage d'obligations parentales'. The growing scarcity of children as well as the rising 'sentimentalization' of parental love (Badinter, 1980) transforms marriage into a 'pedagogical institution' in which many of the rights of the partners are related to their obligations toward (their) children.

Within marriage, parental love thus seems to prevail over the loving bond between partners. Not in the sense that the latter is not important anymore but in the sense that the former should not totally depend upon the latter; parental love remains even where partner love disappears. Both kinds of love develop autonomously and often contest for the mastery.

At the same time, however, more and more parental tasks are taken over by social institutions, from kindergarten to school age child care provisions, from child benefits to committees for juvenile protection. Whilst a family is generally recognized as the optimal network to rear children, families are largely helped in taking up their parental obligations. Generally, one could say that society becomes less and less interested in the fate of partner-relationships, and more and more interested in the fate of the children. (Scarre, 1989)

To say that marriage develops toward a 'parental institution' seems to be at right angles with the tendency to open marriage for non-heterosexual relationships. And indeed, it is strange to observe, on the one hand, more and more heterosexual relations refusing to enter marriage and, on the other, the request of homosexuals to have the possibility to marry. What is, however, in both cases at stake is a *quest for equal recognition.* Non-married couples struggle as much against their discrimination as non-married couples, as non-marriageable couples struggle against their discrimination as non-marriageable couples. In both cases, the reasons are the struggle for equal treatment and treatment as an equal. It is thus remarkable that both remain faithful to *the ideal of monogamy* on the one hand (nobody, to my knowledge, requires that (western) marriages should be possible as well between more than two persons) and to the *ideal of liberty* on the other (no homosexuals, to my knowledge, are pleading for opening a form of marriage to them which is, in itself, closed, allowing for no divorce, nor is anyone pleading for arranged marriages again).

In this sense, legal discourse has had a greater impact on loving relationships than is admitted from a mere passionate perpective. Love's passions are exalted...as long as they respect democratic individuals and the norm of equal respect.

Simultaneously, the postmodern age is in search of a more moderate, not all-devouring, non-possessive, yes, more 'reasonable' kind of love, mainly inspired by feminist writers who deconstructed passionate love in terms of its sexist implications. The very title of Martha Nussbaum's *Love's knowledge* (1990) testifies about this search; it is an attempt to look in western literature for a loving effect that is not irrational, blind, imperialist, anti-social and consumerist. Love and reason can be reconciled.

Does that mean that love and law can meet on less enmical terms? This question remains open for Nussbaum's approach in which priority is given to idiosyncracy, uniqueness and context and in which reason is particularized and does not seem to fit well 'the legal point of view' and its focus on generalized forms of community. This is, at least, the case for the modern conception of law.

Marriage thus remains an intrinsically contradictory institution, just as Luhmann characterized love as '*a totally normal improbalility*'. The relative independency and closeness of social systems and their media in modern society, resulted in the emergence of the individual and the search for a particular inter-individual form of communication.

The more it became possible to develop impersonal social relations in the public sphere, the more the need was felt for more intense personal relations in the private sphere. The cult of privacy is the natural implication of a society in which most interactions lost the need for human communication. (Lipovetsky, 1983)

But the cult of privacy guarantees in no way the possibility of intimacy. Inter-personal encounters lost, in the age of expressive individualism, which glorifies 'spontaneity' and 'sincerity', their traditional interactive structures. They lost any structure - in terms of more or less defined behavioural expectations - altogether. As meetings-without-rules, loving relationships are the real 'relations between strangers' where partners have to start from scratch, even more than business or political relations where at least some codes are still generally accepted.

Ever since Shakespeare's *Romeo and Juliet* the general tendency of loving relationships was toward the rejection of any social, cultural or gender conditions for love, that are not love itself. Love is its own condition and is unconditional. At the same time, love involves the promise of an encounter without codes, a communication without grammar.

This makes these meetings both highly improbable and highly exciting. They express a longing for a community about which the rules - if there are any - are not yet known.

Whilst for long historical periods, the culturally determined rituals of dating and mating (through dancing parties, feasts, celebrations etc.) were generally accepted communicative means, modern society has (particularly during the sixties with its 'cult of authenticity') destroyed many of the codes and rituals which gave sense to gestures, movements, words or deeds.(Raes, 1995) Such traditions were radically rejected by free individuals on the road to their emancipation which 'melted anything solid into air'. Love lost its paradigm or, more exactly, love became the very negation of any paradigm.

In an age wherein 'chosen commitments' take precedence over non-chosen commitments, the possibilities to chose are, however not evidently widened. On the contrary, choosing in a context of unknown codes and unknown others becomes all the more difficult. No wonder that exactly a culture which exalts free choice fosters the creation of more and more 'freely chosen', yet arranged marriages by means of marriage counselling bureaus or particular dating initiatives by professional matchmakers.

The postmodern individual is thus nowadays the only - lonely - animal with no generally accepted mate codes at his or her disposal to communicate his or her intentions. Postmodern society is a 'naked society'. Loving communication became radically undetermined. Perhaps this is the reason why these days, talk about love is so easily transformed into talk about sex and why loving communication is often ridiculed by youngsters who foster the attitude of 'staying cool'. And perhaps this is the reason as well why partners embrace more easily the 'exit' than the 'voice' - option when conflicts arise within their relationship.

As on the market, the exit-option does not require much communication; not satisfied, money back. If a commodity is not what it was expected to be, one simply chooses another one; no questions asked. The voice-option, on the contrary, requires communicative skills, the skill to express one's - good and bad - feelings in face to face communication. But by lack of a culture in which such communication could be embedded, many people opt for the 'silent solution'.

Perhaps legal communication - in all its counterfactuality - is then gratefully accepted, as loving communication seems not to be fit for conflict resolution but only for communication about itself. Law's codes are a very welcome, alienating 'conflict thief' when love's autopoiesis comes to an end. Love can only self-referentially justify itself and is irresponsible for anything beyond it.

It is possible that love will, in the postmodern age, transform into something else, perhaps something more resembling Nussbaum's reasonable love which is inspired by moral feelings as well. A more reflexive, rather than an autopoietic love. But such a communitarian love depicts only one of postmodernism's various paths. There is place as well for a radically irresponsible, 'normless' love which defies, in the age of AIDS, its own survival as in Collard's movie *Les Nuits Fauves* (1991). It is difficult to know what love can mean for a generation which has lost any long term perspective, has to find happiness within the confines of a rather limited 'here and now' and for whom 'the future was nicer'. It is difficult to know what will become of love in an age of diminishing expectations, flexibilization, growing uncertainty and instant satisfaction. The loss of 'great narratives' - including the narrative on 'Love' - has made people more fragile, yet at the same time more brave in confronting one another's disrupted and disrupting ways of life, as is suggested in Yves Simon's novel *La dérive des sentiments* (1991) wherein Marianne and Simon try to 'invent an unusable passion' and are in search of the taste for a stable and solemn love, of which they only find the simulacra from a past age. Perhaps 'finite love' will evolve toward more realistic and less totalitarian engagements as well, exactly because a focus on eternity makes no more sense at all.

8. The relative autonomy of love and law

Is there really a need for any 'reconciliation' between law and love and for a 'harmonization' of love's multiple directions? What could it mean to seek after a more 'passionate law' or a more 'reasonable love'? There is no need to resolve the conflict, for such harmonization would, one way or the other, impoverish both law and love. We should simply accept the tensions between love and law and live with them. If there is a need for legal intervention within loving relationships it should be on legal grounds - that is; grounds of justice - not in the name of love itself. Both 'communicative spheres' have their own telos, their own 'raison d'être'. Why should we always want to get rid of conflicts? Why should conflict itself not be a fundamentally human way of life as well for which there is no 'final solution' available, no stable equilibrium at our disposal? Human beings are not only sensitive beings, able to love, and reasonable beings, able to respect one another; they are also tragic beings, confronted with the impossibility to 'close' their plans of life, as long as they are living. The very possibility to meet another human being, and to fall in love, the very possibility that all previous happiness breaks into pieces because of an encounter entailing another promise of happiness are as much part of our human condition as the possibility that two human beings find an unchallenged continuous gratification in one another.

Human beings are open beings. They may try to 'close' their future, but it is not contrary to their nature if such closure fails. They may try to avoid 'conflicts of the hearth', but they can never guarantee their total rest, unless they stop being sensitive beings.

The very idea that all conflicts are only superfluous and that somewhere 'deep down' something very basic is the solution or the synthesis of all of these conflicts is nothing but a modernistic myth which has made us unarmed to handle conflicts, to live with them.

Marriage is a *legal* relationship, an institution. It involves legal consequences, legal obligations, legal rights. These obligations and rights exist, as legal rights, independent from love. Love and marriage may coincide. There may be love without marriage and marriage without love. But that is not the point; the point is that the *loving* relationship is simply not the law's business. Law belongs to another communicative practice. Law should care for justice between human beings, whether in love or not; it cannot care for or take care of love itself.

Legal identity is, in an important sense, counterfactual. It is not our 'true' identity. But exactly this counterfactuality of law is an important asset in legal communication. (Raes, 1996) Legal communication, based on the idea of individual autonomy and human equality, can be used to challenge subjugation and unjustifiable social relations. The counterfactuality of law defines its limits. Law cannot reflect community, unity or love, but can only reflect and reconstruct some of their implications in its particular language game. The *promise* to confirm legally a loving bond as well as the very *act* to enter marriage may be 'proofs of love', but the legal bond is, in itself, no proof of true love at all.

However, this relative autonomy of love and law needs one important corrective; in both legal and loving communication, interhuman *respect* is a basic value. Both are the heirs of an egalitarian culture, a culture of democratic individualism. (Taylor, 1989) This modern identity has shaped both love and legal relationships, though not in the same sense. In loving relationships respect is a spontaneous feeling for the beloved one as a free human being. Respect arises because one loves and is loved by another autonomous being. Respect between lovers is, according to Sartre (1944) a fundamental though radically contradictory attitude, for lovers aspire at 'possessing another's freedom', which is an impossibility, for either one becomes a mere possession of the other and thereby stops being a free individual or one remains totally free, thereby loosening the lovers' exclusive bond. Yet, even if respect between lovers appears to be based on contradictory aspirations, it is nevertheless as essential to the modern love script as the requirements of authenticity and spontaneity. No love can exist without respect.

Legal respect differs from this in that it does not require any feelings at all and that it enforces interhuman respect or concern, even for our greatest enemies. Legal respect is impersonal, a code of - outer - conduct and nothing more.

But even then and although law has profoundly penetrated affective relationships, it is often impotent to enforce an ethics of equal respect. As long as such respect is part of the spontaneous feelings of partners, no problematic tensions arise, but it often turns the other way. This can be rather disappointing from the point of view of emancipation. Today, the law may have taken sides with raped and battered women, but remains powerless when women, after having been helped by a women home of distress, decide finally to return to their husbands, in the name of 'love'. There is no law against voluntary subjugation in the private sphere.

Law cannot 'express' love, but law need not do that. The identity of lovers is not in the same sense counterfactual. In fact, their communication promises to be nearer the truth and the value of a particular human being. At least in their intentions, lovers aim at meeting one another in their 'total being'. But exactly this 'totalism' of love defines its limits. No society can be based on such communication for practical and intrinsic reasons. No social system can be 'open' and 'total' - and open to total personality - in this sense.

As love defines its scope beyond law and justice, so law defines its scope independent from love. In this sense love and law do not contradict but simply supersede one another's language game, taking account only of their boundaries; the disappearance of love or the superfluity of law. Love and law only touch one anothers' margins. Thus love is accepted as a legitimate reason to marry or to transfer a gift. Here, law simply 'enacts' that the 'reason' is love - though love itself 'has no reasons'. Law does and cannot control it. And even where Belgian judges - and even public officers - gave themselves recently the competence to check the sincerity of marital engagements between Belgians and strangers, they nevertheless can only declare a marriage to be fraudulent ('fake marriages') on the ground of 'external signs' such as whether partners understand one another's language, sleep and live together, know one another's life story. But the judge cannot judge whether people really are 'in love', apart from their saying so. Similarly, in divorce suits, it does not belong to the competence of the judge to say whether people still love one another or not.

Respecting one another's boundaries thus appears to be the best possible marriage between love and law... Clarifying the subtle autonomies and interdependencies which distinguish and relate simultaneously household commitments from parental or loving commitments seems to be urgently required here. Redefining the relative autonomy of the sphere of legal communication and of the sphere of loving communication should thus become the main issue in any postmodern redefinition of partnerships either within or outside marriage. We ought to respect one another's feelings. We ought to respect the requirements of justice and thus the rights of others. We ought to be able to live with the inevitable conflict between love and law, both as lovers and as bearers of individual rights, both as lovers of bearers of individual rights and as bearers of individual rights, confronted with the loss of a beloved one who has fallen in love with another bearer of individual rights. There is no justice in love. There is no love in justice. There is only the recognition that both are fundamental human values, taking precedence under various circumstances, we will never be able to control definitely. Is this tragic, or 'merely' absurd, lacking any sense beyond our senses?

References:

Aubert V. (1965), A note on love, in *The hidden society*, Totowa, New Jersey, 201-235.

Badinter E. (1980), *L'amour en plus. Histoire de l'amour maternel* (XVII-XXe siècle), Gallimard, Paris.

Badinter E. (1986), *L'un est l'autre. Des relations entre hommes et femmes*, Gallimard, Paris.

Bataille G. (1957), *L'érotisme, Minuit*, Paris.

Bellah R. et al. (1986), *Habits of the hearth. Individualism and commitment in American Life*, Harper and Row, New York.

De Beauvoir S. (1949), *Le deuxième sexe*, Gallimard, Paris.

De Rougemont D. (1956), *L'amour et l'occident* (2nd ed.), Plon, Paris.

Dworkin A. (1987), *Intercourse*, The Free Press, New York.

Elchardus M. & P. Heyvaert (1990), *Soepel, flexibel, ongebonden. Een vergelijking van twee laat-moderne generaties*, VUB Press, Brussels.

Elshtain J.B. (1981), *Public men, private women. Women in social and political thought*, Princeton University Press, Princeton.

Elster J. (1986), *Sour grapes. Studies in the subversity of rationality,* Cambridge University Press, Cambridge.

Foucault M. (1976), *Histoire de la sexualité I*, la volonté de savoir, Gallimard, Paris.

Godwin W. (1979), *Enquiry concerning political justice, and its influence on modern morals and happiness,* Penguin, Harmondsworth (1798).

Kierkegaard S. (1943), *Ou bien...ou bien...*, Gallimard, Paris (1843).

Lasch C. (1977), *Haven in a heartless world. The family beseiged,* Basic Books, New York.

Lauritzen P. (1993), *Pursuing parenthood. Ethical issues in assisted reproduction,* Indiana University Press, Bloomington and Indianapolis.

Lipovetsky G. (1983), *L'ère du vide. Essai sur l'individualisme contemporain,* Gallimard, Paris.

Luhmann N. (1976), *Liebe als Passion. Zur Codierung von Intimität,* Suhrkamp, Frankfurt.

MacKinnon C.A. (1987), *Feminism unmodified,* Harvard University Press, Cambridge Massachusetts.

Noddings N. (1984), *Caring. A feminine approach to ethics and moral education,* University of California Press, Berkeley.

Nussbaum M. (1990), *Love's knowledge. Essays on philosophy and literature,* Oxford University Press, New York.

Okin S.M. (1981), 'Women and the making of the sentimental family', *Philosophy and Public Affairs,* 11, 1, 65-88.

Ortega y Gasset (1969), *Über die Liebe. Meditationen,* Deutsche Verlags-Anstalt, Stuttgart.

Paglia C. (1990), *Sexual personae. Art and decadence from Nefertite to Emily Dickenson,* Yale University Press, Yale.

Pateman C. (1988), *The sexual contract,* Oxford University Press, Oxford.

Raes K. (1995), 'Citizenship, public culture and insecurity. A plea for a revaluation of public space', *Ethical Perspectives*, 2, 4, 199-219.

Raes K. (1996), 'Communicating legal identity. A note on the inevitable counterfactuality of legal communication', in Nelken D. (ed.), *Law as communication,* Dartmouth, Aldershot, 3-24.

Sartre J.P. (1944), *L'être et le néant,* Gallimard, Paris.

Shorter E. (1975), *The making of the modern family.* Basic Books,New York.

Scarre G. (ed.) (1989), *Children, parents and politics,* Cambridge University Press, Cambridge.

Taylor C. (1989), *Sources of the self. The making of the modern identity.* Cambridge University Press, Cambridge.

Unger R.M. (1975), *Knowledge and politics,* The Free Press, New York.

Unger R.M. (1984), *Passion. An essay on personality,* The Free Press, New York.

Zelizer V. (1981), *Pricing the priceless child. The changing social value of children,* Basic Books, New York.

Law, Love and the Contestability of European Community

EMILIOS A. CHRISTODOULIDIS

What follows is a defence of a certain philosophical anarchist position (I hesitate to call this, with Thomas Spijkerboor, an 'anarchy of the imagination' for what is an anarchism that renounces praxis?) My purpose is to reinstate a separation between love and law, politics and law and community and law. And I want to claim this disjunction for law *simpliciter,* not merely formalist, positivist or 'eurocentric' conceptions of it. To defend this 'strong' claim I will align the law/love distinction to another, that between the reductive and the reflexive. The reflexive, I will argue, is the horizon of love, the reductive is the horizon of law. All law will be to some extent reductive; if it is not it will not be understood as law and will, in a sense, merge with the world. All love will be, in the last instance, reflexive; if it ceases to question itself it will stagnate and cancel itself out.

I

Think of the confrontation between Pierre and Davout in *War and Peace.*[1] A moment of indecision saved Pierre from being shot as a Russian spy on Davout's orders.

> *Davout looked up and gazed intently at him. For some seconds they looked intently at each other and that look saved Pierre. Apart from conditions of war and law that look established human relations between the two men. At that moment an immense number of things passed dimly through both their minds, and they realised they were both children of humanity and were brothers.*

Commenting on this confrontation Michael Detmold says:

> *Davout, at the moment of practicality entered the unanswering void of particularity, the realm of love, about which only mystical, poetic things can be said or nothing. Lawyers enter this realm every day.*[2]

But if law enters this realm every day it finds nothing there that it can call by name. That is why Davout, faced with his brother Pierre, finds his reasons in love and not in law. Law is already there dictating reasons to act. Pierre is a traitor; the law tells Davout he must kill him. But it is only love that allows Davout to negate his legal duty and encounter Pierre as brother. To law the particularity of the affective encounter is invisible, the particularity could not have pierced the legal terms of its exclusion.

Law is universalistic; even a law of compassion can only ask a universalistic question: how does solidarity require one to act as a rule? But a relationship as complex as solidarity - or 'the social face of love'[3] - appears to resist its reduction to conditional rules, to role requirements; it folds every hypothesis about how one is to act back upon itself. Every action according to the rule needs to be tested as to whether it actually enhances solidarity; and the criteria cannot be provided in abstract. And ultimately every rule as to how one should act in solidarity can be rejected in the name of solidarity itself, tested as to the appropriateness of its application in the here and now. [4] If that is so, no rule or role can relieve the ethical responsibility as it resides in the encounter. This questioning of self, this self-referential quality inherent in solidarity makes its reduction in law an absurdity, the reduction achievement one that collapses as it is questioned.[5] The concept of a *right* to solidarity or love is caught up in an impossible tension, a self-undermining that is not a source of empowerment but a self-cancellation.

Let me elaborate and explain this. To talk about the impossible bridging of the worlds of love and law, I will re-introduce the key terms 'reductive' and 'reflexive' and add a third: self-reference. I will talk a little bit about all three. My additional point is that if they do indeed stand dichotomous, if law and love is a disjunction not a continuum, that we should think also of politics and community as falling on the side of love, not of law. If, that is, we are to do justice to our ability to act in common towards a common future we should not rely on law to perform a task it cannot even give expression to and 'bind' us in a community that elides the particularities of our attachment.

So my position is for a politics that is reflexive like love not reductive like law. Reflexivity is an invitation to think something through, a reduction is a reason not to. I have called something reflexive in that it is not reductive and I must explain this contra-distinction. Reduction means simplification. We live in highly complex societies, the possibilities of communicating they provide are infinite. Over and against the infinite possibilities of communication, modes of discourse develop that provide an adequate way of dealing with the overwhelming complexity, they provide an adequate grasp on great stretches of reality and provide us who inhabit a great many everyday worlds the possibility to understand each other; because we can fix upon a template that reduces the multiple contingency of communication. In this sense the reduction to a template, this coming about of a context, is an important achievement because it simplifies what is overwhelmingly complex. Law is one such template.[6]

This allusion back to grand sociological theory will lead us astray so I will come to the point very quickly through an instance that is of central importance to our theme. It is the question of *collective identity and community*, the question of what holds us together under common self-descriptions. Love is, par excellence, about such commonality, its constitutive moment lies therein. Law too is about this interconnectedness. But it carries a heavy cost associated with its nature as reductive; a cost on how we understand and can potentially contest our collective identity, the possibility of coming together in collective 'we', for present purposes, in 'our' Europe.

The 'we' of politics, like the 'we' of love is reflexive; the 'we' of law, of citizens, of legal persons, is reductive. Where does the contrast lie? between love and law, lover and spouse; between politics and law, political actor and citizen. (I take the symmetry as complete and unproblematical).

In love and politics identity is the emergent property of the relevant interaction. Political praxis forms the context against which collective identity becomes meaningful; through identification with the stakes of that action and against a significant Other whose existence allows recognition and consolidation of collective self-descriptions. Identity is relational and caught up in the forcefield of political contingencies and cannot be abstracted from it. In love, too, relational identity is so cast as to be absorbed into the relationship in a way that uncouples it from any external premise. The world makes sense to the lover in terms of the beloved's experience of it.[7] This reliance on the partner as the mediator between the self and the world[8] radicalizes the relational aspect of the construction of identity. Experience of the world means experience in terms of sharing it, and as everything acquires relevance for the person in terms of this sharing, identity must be conceived as dynamic, as growing through love, ever changing, that is, through the interaction.

Briefly, note how this engages the question of time modalities; how these vary between the legal and loving relationship. Love and marriage operate with different time horizons. Suspended between beginning and end, love controls its own horizon. Love exists only in the 'not yet', ('Die Liebe existiert nur im noch nicht'[9]), one can never have loved enough. Love lies in that promise of future fulfilment, its actual fulfilment signals its end. Love punctuates its time[10] and controls its time; what shows the latter to be especially true is the impossibility of binding love in the time-span of a legal relationship. Binding it externally, attempting to institutionalize permanence, achieves nothing but a semblance of permanence which is intolerable to love. Because love thrives on *change,* its existence over time is dynamic, it requires 'die Formen zu wechseln und immer Neues zu verzehren.'[11] Its structures project enhancement, intensification. In contrast to any legal relationship, immobility is likely to be thematized as indifference, repetition as reluctance to unfold love further, to exceed the limit, which in turn signals the absence of love. Because 'staying is nowhere.'[12]

Similarly, spontaneity and chance play a very different role in love and law. In one sense chance radicalizes the improbabilities on which love relies;[13] introducing chance into what sparks off, maintains and diminishes love, folds love back into an ultimate self-referentiality: no causal input from social structures, no dependence whatsoever on the outside. There is no reason to love other than that one loves. Love's self-referentiality is radicalized through chance and expressed in spontaneity: love's expression cannot be programmed.

II

But consider what complexities this creates. The reflexivity it invites is hardly tolerable; it makes our communities anxious places. We are invited to constantly re-negotiate meanings, re-confirm our bond at every corner of interaction, suspend the fixity of any agreement. But if there is one thing that we associate with law it is the settling of contingency, or at least the reduction of overlapping contingencies to one, the subjugation of divergent dualisms to one: whether something is legal or illegal. Law is about ordering interaction and providing us with some security of expectations. And to order it must simplify. What was dynamic must now be *stilled.*

The 'stilling' is a reduction Conflict, contestation, negotiation will be accommodated at the level of what is expected of one institutionally. Law as an institution entrenches certain reductions in the possibilities of describing and talking about the world, gives us a language to conceive of identity, interdependence, conflict, benefit and harm, concepts of risk and time, what is owed and what is due. These are precisely the kinds of reductions in the possibilities of communicating about the world that make law an institutional achievement. These reductions, Luhmann tells us, occur along the three dimensions of meaning, 'temporal', 'social' and 'material'.[14]

Along the *'temporal'* dimension law reduces uncertainties by furnishing certain expectations and equipping them with 'normativity.'[15] What does this mean? The expectation will produce a legal claim to be tested; the claim will be fulfilled or disappointed and in that will furnish a new expectation of the legal position. Within this schematic account of evolution, there has occurred a transference of 'normativity' between two points in time. What 'transferring normativity' means has to do with how the system handles the disappointment of expectations. Two types of expectation can be differentiated on the basis of how disappointments are handled: *normative and cognitive*. The nature of expectations as normative and cognitive is based on their different ways of 'learning'. Normativity means clinging to expectations despite disappointments. Cognitive expectations on the other hand 'learn' through disappointment. Cognitive expectations change and adapt in cases of disappointment whereas normative expectations do not.[16] Normativity - the transference of disappointment-proof expectations - is one way, but a very important way, in which expectations are 'stilled' and stabilized by the law; it is one way in which complexity comes partially under control.

But law simplifies and reduces things in other dimensions too, 'social' and 'material'. As to the first of these: one of the features of modern law was that it aimed to regulate 'encounters' between strangers[17] and allowed one to abstract one's expectation from the 'concrete' Alter; the personality of Alter ceases to determine the context of expectations and is substituted by Alter-as-role-player. Or, what amounts to the same thing, an expectation becomes legal in that it is assumed to be backed by the expected consensus of third parties who do not know Alter and so must rely only on his capacity as role-taker to form expectations. The introduction of third parties as normatively co-expecting means that the expectation-context is now first abstracted from the concrete interactional setting and first cast through a system-specific referent. Institutionalization thus abstracts into an impersonal context that allows specifically legal attributions of expectations, ones that are normatively co-expected. And how will law make expectation possible? It will have to abstract from specific people's expectations *of* specific people and provide a plane where these expectations can latch on and be attributed to fictitious, but invariant from case to case, units. This is where the abstraction of the legal person becomes operative. The legal personality is such a point of attribution and address.

Finally, along the material dimension, law will give content to the expectation from within a limited pool of possibilities. The creation of a mutuality of expectations is only possible on the basis of a commonality of events, visible action and symbols for the invisible.[18] The infinite possibilities of envisaging events and deciphering them through symbols is reduced though systems like law that provide horizons of other possibilities against which selections can be tested. The world becomes meaningful as legally relevant, through the selectivity, the alignment to referents provided by law. Roles, programmes and values are names for such devices. Through programmes, for example, correctness of behaviour is lifted from the personal context and fixed at the impersonal level, at which level rules ground the normativity of expectation of individual action through impersonal criteria of correctness that displace the personal reference. One can mention here, indicatively, how legal liability is fixed on objective grounds through objective indicators of *mens rea* that are removed from concrete personal capacities of predicting consequences and assessing correctness; or how responsibility is fixed (variably) in various areas of law: family law, tort etc.[19]

In what sense does this discussion of legal reduction in temporal, social and material aspects allow us to probe the difference between law and love in a more precise way? It is because it captures the tensions within and between the meaning of a loving and legal expectation. For example, look at the interplay between the material and the temporal dimensions: role is necessary for identifying the disappointment threshold of the normative expectation. In law as opposed to love, the legal person's expectation will turn normative at the point at which the law designates a disappointment, sanctions an attribution of wrong-doing and provides remedies for the frustrated expectation. On the other hand, in love, as opposed to law, the disappointment threshold varies according to what the lover normatively expects of the concrete Alter - the beloved; this in turn turns on questions of what matters enough, what the expector is ready to concede, overlook or on the other hand be especially sensitive to, all of which can only be answered from within and uniquely about the specific relation. No 'material' objective disappointment thresholds can be set in love, no co-expecting third parties. The normativity threshold is not set through impersonal standards but through interpersonal ones. Only where such disappointment thresholds are fixed through universal and thus impersonal standards can normative expectations be born, and voiced as appropriate to legal relations; but in love the standards are not fixed but retrieved interpersonally. There are other aspects to this interplay of role and normativity. The very differentiation of cognitive and normative depends on whether we are approaching the loving relationship from law or from love. Love is oriented to getting to know the beloved, the world becomes relevant through the beloved. This points to an overwhelming priority of the cognitive and an overwhelming hesitation to switch to normative; i.e. one who loves is always willing to learn from disappointments by shifting expectations. On the contrary, role provides more or less fixed points for the switch from cognitive to normative.[20] This is all to say that the very character of an expectation as cognitive/normative depends on the material dimension for providing the 'switching point'.

While not all legal systems display all the features of reduction I have covered, I claim in defence of my 'strong' position that all legal systems contain at least some form of reduction, along one, at least, of the axes, albeit the allusion to a normatively co-expecting authority, a vocabulary of law, or the commitment to a rule over time. That is why I treat reduction as the horizon of law. Without it law has no distinctive feature to differentiate it from the flux of social interaction. But conceding any reduction at the same time is a concession away from the reflexive, only in terms of which is love possible. Because if law does reduce complexity in these ways, love operates no such facilitating, reductive, 'stilling' factors. No external measure of disappointment or fulfilment can be derived from role; attribution can only be directed to the person, and that means the person as lover. No intermediate-level attributions, here, no avoiding the ultimate questions. No avoiding, that is, reflexive risk.

III

What law destroys, I have claimed, is the reflexivity that is constitutive of love. The legal institution places a wooden hand on love. It denies love the freedom to refer to everything, to problematize everything and to bring everything to bear on its own horizon. Love takes up nothing *a priori*, not the nature of the bond, not the existence of the bond. Love is uncovered, instantiated, re-discovered in every question, every moment of 'ordinary' interaction. On the contrary, law is about blocking this continual reference back to the source. It provides institutional symbols that can be checked against institutional assumptions, inhering in its structures and programmes. In this sense, law is about introducing a prioris, introducing reasons 'not to think about it';[21] because 'the law says so,' because '[Davout's] legal duty dictates it'. Can we really claim law to be the moment that empowers the communal bond? I think not. Because it displaces those very interpretative questions that turn love (like politics) reflexive: turn them upon themselves to ask what they are really about in a way that at once challenges and realizes community. But inserting law as empowering that which love like politics is uniquely suited for, displaces the interpretative questions: it *takes on board community as an a priori by removing from community the ultimate question of what community is; it removes the understanding of what is love, from love.*

What does the argument mean for *the aspiration to contain community in law?* My argument against law and my worry about the legal category 'citizenship' is this: if community is always already in citizenship, we, as citizens, have already accepted the existence and nature of the communal bond and no longer have to 'think about it' and be reflexive about its existence. But this is external, not interpretative and therefore not political. To be political the self-description must remain interpretative, which means leaving open the question of which difference makes the difference to the shaping of identity.

In its continuous questioning of its fulfilment, love substantiated the communal bond, fed questions that constantly brought community to self-conscious realisation. One cannot sever the intimate dialectic between community and love as one cannot sever it between community and politics by imposing law as the mediator. If one is to give politics due significance one has to take the ultimate step back and ask the real question about community: locate in community the understanding of what constitutes community. Radicalizing the question in this way, releasing the variables from legally fixed anchorage points, will create a shifting pattern of communities constellating around understandings that, for the time, seem adequate to hold together people-in-community.

The fragile community exists in articulating its shared commitment, and, significantly, is potentially created and dissolved at every moment of social life because the shared commitment that constitutes it is dynamic, it exists in time. The reflexive argument for what constitutes a community pivots on the 'sharing' and allows the 'what' to be designated reflexively by those whose sharing of it appears significant and adequate to their sense of togetherness. The reflexive is an infinitely delicate process. Community comes about around a political/ethical understanding both capable of upholding a commitment, and dynamic, always potentially disruptable internally: and with no measure of authority, force, persuasion and violence capable of upholding it externally.[22]

And the difference that this definition makes to our discussion of 'law and love in Europe' is this: We 'European citizens' is an a priori. It can, of course, be delimited and thus defined in the mirror of those who are not Europeans. But such are forms of exclusion and they give political aspirations little leverage, and all too often a leverage we abhor. Otherwise than as an exclusionary 'Euro-racism', European citizenship is an a priori circumference of political space. I do not think that it has to be. My suggestion for a reflexive politics could potentially turn the identification 'Europe' into a contested rather than natural setting, and furthermore one where the mode of contestation is in turn contestable. Because solidarities that are significant enough to inform identities form locally and partially, cutting across other political identifications. Our Europe is a multiple Europe, but significantly one that hosts mutually undercutting and mutually denying identifications. I worry about prioritising any of these, reducing them or denying them in the name of community. My worry about law is that as reductive it cannot voice a divergent plurality, one that is internally dissonant, not consonant. Like love, politics as reflexive can tap the seam of the contestability. As a site of political reflexivity, as essentially contested community only, can 'the European community' remain a political aspiration. As such it keeps alive the freedom to contest the terms in which the question of community is contested.[23] Like the distinction between freedom to love and love, that between freedom and politics collapses as it is drawn. Love and politics absorb freedom and elevate it to their constitutive moment. And nowhere as much as in love and politics is it as obvious that what it means to be free is paradoxically tied to the dependencies that love creates.

Notes:

1 Book XII, ch X, quoted in Detmold M, *'Law as Practical Reason'*, [1989] 48, Cambridge Law Journal, p 457.

2 ibid.

3 Unger R, *Law in Modern Society*. New York: Free Press, 1976.

4 Cf. Guenther K, *The Sense of Appropriateness*. Albany: State of New York University Press, 1993.

5 I have elaborated this more fully in 'The Inertia of Institutional Imagination', [1996] 59/3 *Modern Law Review*.

6 I am drawing here on the sociology of Niklas Luhmann. See especially his *Soziale Systeme* (Frankfurt: Suhrkamp, 1984) and more recently and specifically on law: *Das Recht der Gesellschaft* (Frankfurt: Suhrkamp, 1993).

7 Luhmann, *Liebe als Passion*, Frankfurt: Suhrkamp, 1982, p18, ch2 passim and ps 26ff, 219ff.

8 Of Nadja, Breton says: 'Even while I am close to her, I am closer to the things that are close to her' (p104). Nadja herself becomes a sign for shifts of places and things; of Paris where she shifts from quarter to quarter with Breton, and of objects: Nadja's glove, her clothes. What is important is not that these are sites that mediate the intimacy but that they become meaningful through the intimacy they mediate; the world acquires meaning because the beloved inhabits it, and its objects become signs of that love, events increasingly over-invested with meaning as artifices of love.

9 Luhmann, *Liebe als Passion*, p89.

10 In Nadja for example, very little ostensibly happens, sometimes nothing at all, yet the lover-narrator continuously brings events to our attention, momentous events capable of changing his life. These events only come about as he over-invests what happens with meaning. Without love there would have been no punctuation of the continuum, nothing to break or interrupt the flanerie in Paris or the early morning (non-)happenings at the Quai aux Fleurs (in L'Amour Fou).

11 'to change forms, and always to consume something new.' (Luhmann, Liebe als Passion, pp90-1).

12 'Wie der Pfeil die Sehne besteht, um gesammelt im Absprung mehr zu sein als er selbst. Denn Bleiben ist nirgends' Rilke, *Duineser Elegien*, 8.

13 This openness to risk is most prominent in Nadja. The submission of love to risk, to danger or to endless possibility, (or to both as in the book's final chapter's footnoted incident), is elevated here to nothing less than the condition of a love that is because it is in risk, a love that - as always tentative (never yet accomplished) - demands more risk, and love that absorbs all risk by defining what risk means self-referentially.

14 See Luhmann N: *The Sociological theory of Law*. Translated by E King-Utz and M Albrow. London: Routledge and Kegan Paul, 1985 [original: Rechtsoziologie, 1972].

15 'In a way that no other system does, the law processes expectations that are capable of maintaining themselves in situations of conflict.' (Luhmann, '*Law as a Social System*', in 83, Northwestern U L R, 136, 140).

16 This of course is not absolute; as Luhmann points out normative expectations exceptionally learn as when the law provides procedures for its own change or when the elasticity of legal structures prompts judge-created law. On the other hand cognitive expectations do not always learn as when a disappointment is classified as an exception to the rule; not every slight deviance from the expected results leads to a paradigm shift in science.

17 I owe this point to Koen Raes.

18 Luhmann explains that 'the expectation of expectations is only possible through the mediation of a common world to which expectations are identically attached' (*The Sociological theory of Law*, p62).

19 As the law evolves, roles, programmes and values shift and, what is more striking, their interplay and interdependence shifts. The rise, for example, of formal rationality and the uprooting of legal relations from their Gemeinshaft context, as well as the reversal of this evolutionary trend in the era of the Welfare State is reflected in a mutually re-inforcing re-negotiation of values (certainty and justice) a shift in programming (a retreat of conditional and an expanse of goal programming) and a 're-materialisation' of roles (from the all-inclusive legal personality to more concrete loci of attribution of rights and duties).

20 'I need not inquire into your motives deeper, there are laws for spouses that act as you do!'. Ego's expectation of Alter is not qualified in the light of Alter's action to expect something new next time, but is disappointed instead (normative not cognitive); the law designates what actions have this effect, and reads in this not only a disappoinment of a right in law but one that re-enacts a disappointment of the love Ego had invested.

21 See Bankowski Z, 'Don't Think About It: Legalism and Legality'. In Karlsson M et al (eds): *Law, Justice and the State*. Berlin: Duncker & Humblot, 1993.

22 To paraphrase Robert Cover, the spontaneous orders of the diverse nomoi, the reflexive diversity, cannot survive its passage into state law. The courts' authority, he says, comes from a unique power to deny other meanings. (Cover, R '*Violence and the Word*', in 95, Yale L J, pp1601).

23 This is to secure a space for ambiguity in democratic politics so as to prevent political practice from reproducing discourses of control, perpetuating closure around stable patterns. The first moment of reflexivity - that of upsetting settled meaning - is well captured in deconstruction. The idea of the essential contestability of concepts is relevant to a thesis of reflexive politics. The main idea here is that concepts are not (what Lyotard would call) 'rigid designators' but are themselves politically negotiable, and thus are aspects of the reality they help shape. Connolly says 'to examine and revise the terms of political discourse is not a prelude to politics but a dimension of politics itself.' (*The Terms of Political Discourse*. Lexington, Massachussets: Heath, 1974, p3).

Family Reunification: Who Pays for Love in Europe?

MARIE-CLAIRE FOBLETS

"L'amour est enfant de bohème,
il n'a jamais connu de loi [...]"
'Carmen', Georges Bizet

1. Introduction

The argument of my paper builds upon a somehow 'disenchanting' statement. It is the statement that love and love relations that fall under the jurisdiction of EC Law are not protected as a value in itself, but as a requirement for productivity gains. EC law makes the right to install oneself with a beloved person conditional on a means test. The very question is *who can afford for the cost of that love and for the kind of human relations it engenders*. I will develop my argument in relation to family issues involving non-EC nationals, so called 'Third Country Nationals' (TCN's).

One fortuitous example of love relations involving both EC and non EC nationals will conduct the exposé.

> Two boys, *Marco* and *Youssef*, both between 20-25, share a small appartment in Paris.
> *Marco* is Italian and serves in a small bar downtown. His friend *Youssef* is the youngest child of Algerian parents who have lived for over 30 years in France. He is partially disabled, crippled in a car accident. Due to his handicap he cannot afford to live on his own. He therefore shares an appartment with *Marco*. At the age of 18 years, *Youssef* was granted French citizenship. Because of his handicap he was never offered the opportunity to take up a job. He is still waiting to be recognized for individual social security.

For *Marco*, life in Paris is extremely stressful. For *Youssef*, life is just too expensive. Both boys therefore most often spend their holidays together, usually in France occasionally abroad. On a trip in Spain both of them fall in love with *Fatiha*, a Moroccan girl, whom they met in a coffeeshop in the neighborhood of Barcelona. Each of them very eagerly wishes to start a relationship with her and, with some luck, take *Fatiha* with him to Paris.

The question in connection with the topic of my paper is the question who of the two boys, conforming to EC Law is in the position to be the winning lover. For the purposes of the illustration I will have to make abstraction of the girl's feelings ... It may sound odd, indeed.

Before puzzling together the answer, building on the interplay between the principle of freedom of movement of persons under EC law and the French legislation on 'family reunification',[1] I owe the reader some background information on the way family questions, traditionally, are being dealt with under EC Law: *what is Europe's love-policy*?

1. EC Law treatment of family relations

It is commonplace that EC law (now European Union's law) is 'market law', designed with the purpose of promoting the cross-border functioning of market operations *within the Union.*[2] The main area of concern of the European institutions, for at least 30 years, has been the completion of one single goods market (both production and consumption) i.a. through the consolidation of labour standards: wage-policies; improvement of health and safety *at work*; equal treatment of men and women *on the labour market*, etc... fit in a perspective of broad economic priorities.

Family life and love relations in that logic are not the point. The very interest of the European institutions in issues dealing with love and intimacy between indivuals is economic. I will restrict the illustration of that statement here to the issue of *family reunification*. Family reunification under EC law allows certain categories of relatives the right to install themselves with a person whose freedom of movement derives directly from the Treaties, originally the EEC-Treaty and by now also the Treaty on the European Union.[3] It shapes the freedom of movement of the family members of an EC national who is himself a trainee, a worker under contract or a worker in regular employment in the territories of the Member-States. It includes besides the right to install oneself with the holder of the original right to freedom of movement, a right to remain permanently in the host State, admission to normal education on the same conditions as the nationals of that State, the right to take up work and benefits under the social security system of that State. However, family reunification as *such* is not a concern of the EC construction. Interference with family ties under EC jurisdiction issues from considerations that are in the first place economically grounded. The purpose of the EC regulations concerning family reunification is to facilitate economic integration via the promotion of the mobility of workers in the Community. Neither the right to respect of family life, nor the right to found a family is explicitly chosen as a fundamental principle of EC law. It is only because a full prohibition on employees to have their families joining them in the country of employment is expected to obstruct the further development of one integrated labour market, that working people are to be entitled to a truly social life, *including the benefits of family intimacy*. The underlying rationale is that if workers were not allowed to have their families accompanying them, many of them - at least those who lead a happy family life - would most probably abandon all ambitions to be employed abroad. Such would hinder the further integration of the European market. The ECJ (European Court of Justice) has consistently declared that disadvantages faced by migrant workers from other EC Member-States, who are to leave their country and their family, vis-à-vis a national worker could act as an obstacle to mobility. In other words, family life, from a European point of view, is mainly being looked at as a possible impediment, an obstacle to the competitiveness of the Community market as a whole: it's men's and women's capacity as workers that matters, not their aptitude to love and tenderness.[4] Family life being interpreted as an extension of that priority, not the other way around. Freedom of movement includes the right to be treated on an equal footing with nationals of the host country as regards the right to love with one's immediate relatives.

Since a few years the same 'EC way of regarding love' applies to categories of EC nationals who are not immediately linked to the labour market. In 1990 the Council had indeed adopted three Directives on the right of residence in Member-States for three categories of persons: students, pensioners and EC nationals who have never been economically active.[5] Over the years, as the European population is aging and international mobility ever increasing, unavoidably new problems linked to the protection of cross-border family life and intimate relations have occurred. Since 1990 the Council has been trying to bridge some of the gaps between the treatment, on the one hand, of love relations involving at least one economically active person ('worker') and, on the other hand, between persons who are not or no longer occupationally active. What is to become under EC law of intimate relations and family life situations of categories of EC nationals who are not occupationally active on the labour market? Over the last 20 years, the numbers of adult people who fall under that category has been impressively increasing.

By now thus the Council has granted protection to the love relations of three additional categories of persons: students, pensioners and those who have never been occupationally active.[6] EC law provides these three categories of EC nationals with the right to live in other Member-States, even if they are not economically active.

As concerns pensioners for instance, two situations may occur. *Either* the worker has accumulated a number of years of work, in the host state: he then is entitled to stay with his or her family - for the mere reason that he or she has already contributed to the social security system in the host state, both for him- or herself and for the family. *Or* a worker wants to make use, *after retirement*, of the right to freely move throughout Europe and moves to a better place within the territories of the Member-States.[7] Since 1990, the Directive[8] compels Member-States to open their national borders to retired people, under the very condition however that the candidating persons are in the position to pay for themselves and for their family the costs of their cross-border mobility. Retired people are thus entitled to make use of the right to travel freely within the Community, both for themselves *and for their family* in as far as they can prove to be already beneficiary of the social security system in the home country or in any other social security system: i.e. that they can prove to be already contributing somewhere to the social security system and during a sufficiently long period of time.

Some authors have vividly criticised this very selective 'open borders' policy within Europe for allowing solely the happy few, the elite, those who can afford paying for the liberty to move and settle, to love and be joined by their beloved relatives at their best conveniences.[9] A policy of granting the right to family reunification only to better off EC nationals reinforces the idea that there is a group of second-class individuals in Europe who, for not being in the capacity to pay for the consequences of their feelings, are denied the right to stable cross-border relations.

The same 'love-under-condition-of-credit-worthiness' policy has been adopted for regulating the protection of family life of *students* throughout Europe.[10] Originally students were not allowed to circulate freely in the Community and pursue their education abroad, except if they were able to prove that the chosen education was directly linked to the improvement of their competitiveness on the labour market.[11] At first, these students had to pay for their studies abroad. Starting from the late 70s however, Member-States have been compelled by the ECJ to pay for the studies of European students in their own universities and grant them the same regime as the one enjoyed by their own nationals.[12] By now, Directive 93/96[13] provides for a right of residence in other Member-States for the purposes of pursuing a vocational training course. By virtue of the Directive, European students are now allowed to reside with their families in the country of their education, in as far as they can pay for the costs of living: they have to be covered by a health insurance in their own country or in any other country, *previously to their arrival.* The residence permit is limited to the duration of the studies. The result of this type of regulation may be odd. Practically, as studying abroad anyhow is more expensive than studying in one's home country, the above mentioned critique here also applies: since the Directive on the right of residence for students, the right of students to love 'cross-borderly' during their studies (by freely moving with their family within the territories of the Member-States) has officially become a privilege for the better off.

These illustrations should suffice here. They show that the effectiveness of the EC legislation (case law, directives, etc.) on free circulation within the territories of the Member-States comes, in the first place, to a system that has been elaborated to provide for the necessary systems of control and sanctions that warrant economically *profitable* migration movements, and lay a severe prohibition - via the condition of financial self-support - on all others forms of cross-boundary intimate relations. The statement applies in particular to the category of EC nationals who are not occupationally active. In effect these persons, as long as they cannot prove sufficiently wealthy, are hindered from the benefit of the right (guaranteed by art. 8a of the Treaty) to move and reside freely within the territories of the Member-States. Unemployed people, who are in many cases not allowed to export their unemployment allocation and people who live on social benefits (e.g. disabled people), are the first victims of the 1990 Directives.

The 'EC way of conceiving love' and the protection of love relations, with even more restrictions, also applies to family relations involving TCNs. The principles encompassing the right to family reunification involving TCNs have been elaborated in treaties, both in regulations and directives and in the case-law of the ECJ [14] that define the groups of TCNs who can be considered as 'persons' under Article 3 EEC-Treaty,[15] entitled to have their relatives accompanying them.

2. Additional restrictions to the family reunification with TCNs

The logic that applies to the free circulation of workers and their families *within* the European Communities since 1958,[16] is basically the logic that has been applied by the Member-States individually, starting from the 60s and 70s, in negotiating labour immigration treaties (mainly bilateral treaties) with third countries such as Morocco, Algeria, Tunisia and Greece, previously to its joining to the European Community[17]: *Family reunification* with relatives from third countries has been allowed with the view to encourage candidating emigrants to leave - together with their relatives - their country of origin and come and work in Europe. The same logic, still, applies to the agreements negotiated by the Community itself with non member countries.[18] Several agreements make provision for the way in which Member-States treat family relations betweens TCNs. The right of TCNs to accept an actual offer of employment in one or even several Member-States has been extended to the right to family reunification. The right to love and intimacy between TCNs is enshrined in the 'worker's' rights. It appears from the interplay between the international agreements and the national immigration laws of most Member-States that the right of TCN's to love and engage is restricted by a few significant additional conditions that are worth mentioning here:

In most European Member-States today, the right for TCNs to reunify with their family is reserved to the persons *who can afford financing family life* on the territory of the host country. Only he or she who proves that he (or she) is sufficiently resourceful is granted the protection of his or her family life under the jurisdiction of the host state. The right of TCNs to install oneself with his or her family derives from primary rules as to the capacity to provide adequate accomodation (i.e. a sufficiently roomy house), to support the costs of the education of the children, and thirdly, to finance health insurance of the newcomer(s).

As to the other conditions, the regulations may differ from Member-State to Member-State. Some host countries require a minimum period of residence of the first holder of the permit, i.e. the person who has already been granted residence before family reunification is permitted. Most States refuse permission for the spouse to enter if the State considers that the marriage was contracted solely or principally for the purpose of enabling the spouse to enter that State. The same applies to adoption: most States refuse adopted children the right to enter the State, if the State is of the opinion that the adoption has been arranged solely for the purpose of enabling the child to enter the State. With regard to children each State fixes a maximum age (between 16 and 18 years): after the children have reached that age, they are no longer granted permission to reunify with their family in Europe. In most States, under certain conditions children born from a previous marriage of a legally resident TCN are also admitted. Furthermore, some States examine if the criteria for admission, as laid down for first admission, are still fulfilled when the (temporary) validity of the first permission expires. Finally, States can refuse entry to family members of TCNs if they constitute a threat to national security, public policy (e.g. the second or third wife of a polygamous husband) and on grounds of public health.

On the whole family reunification granted to TCNs is far less generous than family reunification granted to EC citizens. The spouses and the children of TCNs are usually admitted only for the purpose of living continuously together with them and only for the duration of the residence permit of the first holder. The case law of the ECJ concerning the interpretation of marital relationships betweens EC nationals is less restrictive. Practising lawyers may remember the ECJ's rather flexible interpretation of the term 'spouse' in the *Diatta* case[19]: a Senegalese national, married with her French husband who lived and worked in Berlin, was refused a prolongation of her residence permit because of her living separately from her husband and of her intention to divorce him. The ECJ considered that EC law[20] does not require that the member of the family in question lives permanently with the worker: '[...] *A requirement that the family must live under the same roof permanently cannot be implied'*.

The consequence of the *Diatta* decision is that even marriages involving EC nationals of which the existence continues only for the convenience of the advantages of EC law seem to allow family reunification. A survey of the case-law of the ECJ devoted to the interpretation of 'family life' involving EC nationals is illuminating: all kinds of arrangements between married people - involving living together and apart - are being granted the protection of family life and thus family reunification. In the Court's view national borders cannot affect the relationships between married couples involving at least one

EC national - who is either occupationally active or sufficiently supportive (*cf. supra*) -, even if the spouses do not intend effectively sharing everyday life in common. Conforming to the Court, the frequency and the ease with which both parties in the *Diatta* case criss-crossed Europe, is at all costs to be encouraged.

TCNs on the contrary, so far are not allowed to 'live apart together' cross-borderly in Europe: the protection of family life granted to EC nationals living apart is withheld from couples of TCNs, *even to couples in stable relationships*. The discrimination wouldn't be that significant if the numbers of couples of TCNs who have to cope with the discrimination, were less important. In Europe today, the majority of all foreigners resident within the European Union are not citizens of other Member-States, but are nationals of other countries. The statistical data for the population of lawfully resident TCNs varies from between 8-9 million to 13 million, which is greater or equivalent to the populations of some of the individual Member-States. The numbers are of considerable importance as they demonstrate that a significant number of lawfully resident foreign nationals are excluded from the benefits of a development which, since the *Diatta* case, by allowing residence to spouses, even if they live permanently under separate roofs,[21] extends considerably the group of protected love relations involving EC nationals.

3. Discriminations between EC nationals and between EC nationals and TCNs in matters relating to family reunification

At the basis of the discrimination between treatment (by national authorities or law courts) of family reunification involving EC nationals and treatment of reunificiation of TCN's partners, lies the conviction of still the vast majority of EC law practitioners that there is no unjustified distinction between nationals of Member-States (and those of other States) and TCNs lawfully resident in a Member-State. In the past, the European Commission has urged for a research on the pros and cons of the abolition of that distinction.[22] At present, as I have already mentioned, as far as family reunification is concerned, EC law still gives the opportunity to discriminate against TCNs vis-à-vis EC nationals.

The consequences of this are well illustrated through the answer to the question whether - concretely - in the above mentioned case *Fatiha*[23] qualifies as belonging to the category of persons allowed to accompany their lover and under which conditions she might be allowed to join either *Marco* or *Youssef*.

To properly answer the question who of the two boys, *Marco* or *Youssef*, is entitled under EC law to offer to *Fatiha* any future whatsoever in France, one has to distinguish between two types of discrimination in matters relating to 'family reunification' within the territory of the (European) Member-States.

The first type of discrimination concerns a very peculiar discriminatory treatment among EC nationals. Until the approval of the above mentioned 1990 Directives, EC nationals were entitled to claim the right for their family members to reunify with them *only in as far as they themselves had already made use of the right to freely move* from the territory of one Member-State to another - or several other - Member-State(s), by having accepted an offer of employment abroad, either in the present or in the past (in the case of pensioners or of unemployed 'workers'). That principle - at least partially - still holds. It implies that individuals who claim the right under EC law to have their relatives come over and live with them in another Member-State, first have to prove that they are themselves a national of one Member-State *who is - or has been - employed in the territory of another Member-State*. It is only since the Directives of 1990[24] that also students, pensioners and, more generally, EC nationals who have never been economically active, are equally allowed to claim the right to family reunification for their relatives, as far as they pass the means test (*cf. supra*).

In effect, the EC rationale in matters relating to love and the protection of intimate relations leads to a system of protection of family relations that, paradoxically, is far more generous for EC nationals *who have moved to another EC Member-State* than the protection granted to relatives under forum law. In the example, *Marco* who is a national of a Member-State (Italy) and who is employed in the territory of another State, derives the right under EC law to claim protection of his feelings for *Fatiha* directly from Article 10 of Regulation 1612/68.[25] His position as candidate fiancé therefore is much more likely than the position of *Youssef* to make him (*Marco*) become the successful lover: it will suffice to claim for recognition of his right as an Italian citizen who resides as a 'worker' in another Member-State to be entitled to marry the girl and have her living in France - either with him or apart[26] - *via the permission to family reunification*. He will be able to keep his job in Paris notwithstanding the fact that he fell in love abroad. *Youssef* on the contrary is less fortunate. In application of the Council Directive of 1990 on the right of residence for those who have never been economically active,[27] *Yous-*

sef might be allowed to claim family protection under EC law, notwithstanding the fact that he has never been occupationally active. The problem however is that he never made use of his right to freely move within the Community: he remained in France and will therefore be subject to the French regulations on family reunification.[28] Neither his French nationality nor the means test - for being still dependent on his parents' health insurance it is predictable that he would not pass that test - will suffice to make the Council Directive of 1990 applicable to his claim. At this stage, he is depending on French immigration laws to be allowed to have the girl come over to live with him.

This brings me to the second category of discriminations in the realm of family reunification under EC law which may as well be illustrated by means of a further analysis of the data of the case of *Marco, Youssef* and *Fatiha*. It concerns the differential protection of family ties involving EC nationals and family relations among TCNs.

Imagine *Youssef*, born in France but from Algerian parents, had kept his Algerian nationality, without cumulating his first citizenship with the nationality of the host state. He then would be a TCN. His lover's situation would be even weaker. As a 'foreigner' he would have to rely on the conditions imposed in France - by the French immigration laws - on lovers who *both* originate from third countries. On the whole, these rules concerning family reunification with TCNs are extremely restrictive.[29] As I have already mentioned the regulations regarding family reunification with TCNs differ from Member-State to Member-State. The right to family reunification with TCNs is usually formulated in restrictive provisions, unsuitable to guarantee non-discrimination between TCNs and EC nationals. It is only since the discussion on the *European 'Resolution on Harmonization of Family Reunification'*, adopted at the Copenhagen meeting in 1993, that the EC Member-States have started agreeing on common standards of protection of family ties with TCNs.[30] The Resolution enumerates a few principles[31] concerning family reunification with TCNs, lawfully resident within the territory of the Member-States on a basis that affords them an expectation of permanent or long-term residence. The Resolution however, is not legally binding on the Member-States and does not afford a ground for action by individuals. But even if it were enforceable, it still gives Member-States the opportunity to discriminate against TCNs vis-à-vis EC nationals. The principles of protection that apply under the Copenhagen Resolution to family ties with TCNs on the one hand and between EC nationals on the other hand, are still much more flexible and tolerant to the second category of relations.

The discrimination is twofold. The first discrimination has already been mentioned. It concerns the obligation for the TCN's partners to cohabit. If *Fatiha* were to choose *Marco*, she would be granted permission to reside in France, with some chance even if she and *Marco* were not effectively intending to cohabit on a continuous base. *Youssef*, on the contrary will have to live permanently together with *Fatiha* if she is to stay in France on the sole base of the marriage contracted between them. The condition that the spouse (and the children, if any) may only be admitted for the purpose of living continuously *together*, still holds under the Copenhagen rules. The second discrimination has to do with the very grounds on which a residence permit has been delivered to the first holder of the residence permit on the territory of a Member-State. If the girl were to migrate to Belgium for example, one of the conditions *Youssef* would have to satisfy is the very peculiar condition[32] that he may not himself have immigrated to Belgium through family reunification (e.g. he would have joined his father at a very early age, together with the mother, after having spent the first years of his life in Algeria). The condition does not hold for *Marco*.

The conclusion sounds odd: love relations under EC law are all but spontaneous. Family ties are given an instrumental reading. Family immigration policies under EC law not only privilege family ties of persons with 'market connection', so far they have also neglected protection of cross-border relations that fit in an evolutionary and dynamic interpretation of family life: thus, for instance, neither the right of residence for unmarried and/or homosexual partners,[33] nor the right of residence for elderly parents with their children[34] are laid down so far in EC regulations.

In sum, family and love relations under EC law are mainly to be considered part of the employee's status, social situation and supply conditions. As I have already tried to show, the very target of the legislation concerning the protection of cross-border family ties with those who are 'persons' under EC law, i.e. who avail themselves of freedom of movement, is the promotion of international economic integration. To love someone abroad is all but an evidence under EC law as long as the partners cannot prove either their immediate utility for the economy of the country of residence, or their individual capacity to provide for themselves and their family, without having to burden public funds. Feelings of love between the partners are irrelevant, or at least of secondary importance, in view of these objectives. This rationale leads to a system of differentiated entitlements to love relations based on criteria that mean nothing to loving beings.[35] The Governments of the Member-States however will have to realize that people, universally, are loving beings, capable of feeling very intense attraction and tenderness for one another, *irrespective of age, sex or nationality* and that they undoubtedly will keep on being that way *notwithstanding the economic calculus, the costs and benefits analysis that is being imposed upon them.* That very propulsion of people, the human search for protection of cherished relations in one's life, has most probably a lot to do with the 'success' since a few years among TCNs of the *European Convention on Human Rights and Fundamental Freedoms (1948).*

4. The protection of fundamental rights

An alternative approach to look at the legal status of cross-border love relations, involving TCNs, is through the concept of fundamental human rights. The ECJ has repeatedly held that '[...] *the fundamental human rights form an integral part of the general principles of Community law, the observance of which is ensured by the European Court of Justice'.*[36] These rights are anchored in the Constitutions of the different Member-States and further in different international treaties upon which Member-States have collaborated or to which they are signatories. One of these international treaties is the *European Convention on Human Rights and Fundamental Freedoms* (ECHR). All European Communities Member-States are also members of the E.C.H.R. that applies (1) to all, as soon as they fall under the jurisdiction of any of the Members to the Convention, *irrespective of nationality (TCNs included) and (2) irrespective of any 'market connection'.*

Discriminatory treatment regarding family reunification raise questions under three articles of the Convention *which protect family ties*: Article 8 ECHR on the 'right to respect for private and family life', article 12 ECHR on the right to marry and found a family and article 14 ECHR which prohibits discrimination relating to restrictions on the rights and freedoms defined in the Convention. What makes these articles all the more interesting is the very fact that the protection of the Convention applies, as I mentioned, *irrespective of the nationality.* Thus, family ties and love relations among TCNs that are denied admission under EC law, may still fall under the protection of the fundamental rights defined in the Convention.[37] The nationality of the partners is not relevant in that respect: they may be EC nationals or TCNs. Both the case-law of the European Commission and the Court of Human Rights, and that of the ECJ so far have been shown quite effective at strengthening the protection of family ties among TCNs in Europe. The ECHR does not contain a general right of admission into and residence in a Member-State for TCNs, nor does it contain a prohibition of expulsion of TCNs.[38] However, there are certain provisions in the Convention which, on their own or in conjunction with one of the other provisions, imply elements which may be directly related to such a right and prove useful in terms of protection of family ties.

The protection of Article 8[39] in particular appears to be of vital importance for the protection of law and family relations among TCNs and is often combined with the claim for equal treatment provided for in article 14 of the Convention. Both articles have proven to be extremely precious to compensate for the vulnerability of family members who, not possessing the nationality of one of the European Member-States, are not granted protection of their family ties under EC law and cannot claim either the protection provided for by an international agreement (labour immigration treaties, etc.). Articles 8 and 14 ECHR are often used as an ultimum remedium (ultimate remedy), i.e. when no other law, directive, rule, resolution or court decision any longer guarantees the protection of the family ties involved. It is so haphazard that the European Court of Human Rights since a few years has started developing an impressive body of case law related to the protection of family ties among TCNs.

In at least ten cases in which family ties could not otherwise have been protected, the European Court of Human Rights has granted TCNs the right to join relatives (spouses, parents) who were lawfully resident within the territories of the Member-States, *considering the fundamental right of family life requires admission to the State and prohibits subsequent expulsion.*

I have selected here three decisions that, for the purposes of my exposé, illustrate the Court's jurisprudence. The Court so far has shown to be more inclined to grant protection to family situations involving TCNs lawfully resident in a Member-State territory *that are already existing and have proven stable* and less inclined to protect family relations that are not yet institutionalized, that are still to come into existence (for instance, between fiancés).

4.1. The protection of the establishment of (new) family life

The *Abdulaziz* case[40] involved a number of foreign women who were lawfully established in the United Kingdom, but whose husbands were not permitted to have residence there. *In each case, man and wife had not yet lived together.* The Court held that the extent of a State's obligation to admit relatives of settled immigrants into its territory varies according to the particular circumstances of the persons involved. It was not shown in the *Abdulaziz* case that there were obstacles *to establish family life in the home countries (in casu*, non Member-States) of either the wives or the husbands. Therefore, the Court did not find a lack of respect for the right of family life in the United Kingdom's refusal to admit the husbands to the country where the wives were lawfully living.[41]

4.2. The protection of stable and long lasting family relations

The case of *Berrehab* concerned the expulsion of a divorced husband whose child stayed with his former wife. Mr. *Berrehab* saw his daughter four times a week for several hours at the time. The Court held that cohabitation is not a necessary condition of family life between parents and minor children. The relationship created between the spouses by a lawful and genuine marriage has to be regarded as 'family life'. A child born of such union is *ipso facto* part of that relationship. The Court took into account that Mr. *Berrehab* had lived for several years in The Netherlands, had a home and a job there, and that no complaint had ever been brought against him. The Court concluded that the interest of the individual outweighed the interest of the Dutch State.

The case of *Moustaquim*[42] concerned an immigrant of the second generation, *Abderrahman Moustaquim* emigrated from Morocco to Belgium when he was one year old. For the rest of his life he lawfully lived in Belgium. Three of his seven brothers and sisters were born there. One of his elder brothers held Belgian nationality. While Mr. *Moustaquim* was still a minor, many charges of theft and five charges of robbery were brought against him. For several periods he was detained in a juvenile prison. After his 18th birthday he was again prosecuted and sentenced to two years of imprisonment. After serving his prison sentence he was to be expelled from Belgium.

The question presented to the Court was whether the expulsion of a person from a country where he had virtually lived all his life with his family to a country where he knew neither the culture, nor the language, was an infringement of the right to respect for one's family life. The Court held that there was an interference with the right to respect for family life. The Court pointed to the fact that *Moustaquim* had never broken off relations with his parents and brothers and sisters. The Court found that the family life of *Abderrahman Moustaquim* was affected. Accordingly, the Court found a violation of the applicant's right of respect for his family life.

The rapidly increasing number of cases brought before the European Court of Human Rights by TCNs who fear infringement of their right to respect for their family life demonstrates the need for a legal framework for objective control over Member-States' policies regarding the protection of love- and intimate relations involving TCNs resident in their territory.

In the case of *Youssef, Marco* and *Fatiha*, the right for *Fatiha* to enter France with the view to establish herself with Youssef is not as such guaranteed by the ECHR. In the interpretation of the Court in the *Abdulaziz* case, there is no obligation whatsoever for the French authorities to admit *Fatiha* into the French territory to allow her to *establish a new family situation* (considering she intends marrying *Youssef*). On the contrary, in case she would prefer a relation with *Marco*, her claim to reunify with her fiancé in France, under the condition of a subsequent marriage, would fall under the protection of EC law and be considered favourably. She would then not even need to claim the protection of the ECHR.

5. Conclusion

Should we conclude thus, that EC law and love relations are incompatible with one another, in particular as far as TCNs are concerned?

What should it take to strengthen the protection of love and tenderness in the face of economic necessities? The core attribute of human - men and women - identity, namely the very capacity to love and engage, freed from the divisions of nationality would no longer follow the boundaries of national States and their economic rationale. The changes to bring about such a European 'love'-policy would, no doubt, be vast. But they are not unimaginable. First, the Community institutions should harmonize the legal and administrative regulations and relevant Members-States' measures. Second, EC law should ensure that the conditions for implementing the free movement of TCNs are laid down on the same footing as for EC nationals.

It could of course be objected that changes of this magnitude by far transcend the legitimate concerns and the competence of EC law. So far, EC law has understood cross-border relations of love and attachment between people and *a fortiori* family reunification as the repository of technical rules which affect but formal, non-substantive dimensions of intimate relations. The legal fixation on the status of wealth and economic 'utility' of the partners entrenches family ties in an understanding of lovers as primarily 'occupationally active' people. Love and love relations, not being part of economic life, are considered to lay outside the ambit of the Community power.

However, ultimately EC law claims to be based on social justice and moreover, social justice as a fundamental right.[43] In the legal culture of western Europe, social justice refers to efforts to create equal rights. In the field of love and the protection of human attachment, what counts is that all individuals lawfully resident in the territories of the Member-States, both EC nationals and TCNs, are given proportionate access to love and human intimacy. The salient point for that argument is that continued inequality between TCNs and EC nationals in the core field of love and love relations between men and women constitutes a perversion of Community principles and, on a number of points, is contrary to the logic of the internal market which underlies the free movement of persons within the territories of the Member-States. Love and love relations, irrespective of nationality, are at the heart of the open European society. Their protection needs to be reformulated by legal arguments that do not use these relations for devious ends or to cloak vested economic interests. Love relations involving TCNs today occupy a position of paradigmatic significance in the European integration process.

Notes:

1 For an introductory comment on the French legislation regarding family reunification, see i.a.: Rapport de M. J.-P. PHILIBERT sur le projet de loi (no267) relatif à la maîtrise de l'immigration et aux conditions d'entrée, d'accueil et de séjour des étrangers en France, sur les propositions de loi nos 37,49,50,104,132, et annexe à propos des observations présentées au nom de la Commission des Affaires Etrangères saisie pour avis par M.J. MYARD, Assemblée Nationale no 326 en date du 10 juin 1993.

2 The key objective of the Communities, and later on the Union (cf. infra note 3), has been - from the very beginning in 1958 - to ensure that through the creation of one single market (one market for steel and coal; one market for goods and services; and finally, one market for the circulation of people linked to the labour market: employees, employers, tradesmen; and today, even: tourists, students, and consumers largely defined); that the creation of such a single market would lead to the 'integration' of labour standards, improve competition and - on the long term - ensure that working class people within Europe could share in the new prosperity.

3 The Treaty on the European Union (TEU) which was signed at Maastricht (The Netherlands) on February 7, 1992, creates one European Union out of the three separate European Communities (the European Coal and Steel Community; the Atomic Energy Community and the European Economic Community. On that treaty, see i.a.: O'KEEFFE, D., TWOMEY, P.M. (eds.), *Legal Issues of the Maastricht Treaty*, London, Chancery Law Publishing, 1994; CARTOU, L., ROUX, X., 'Maastricht: commentaires du traité de l'Union européenne', *Actualités communautaires*, extrait no 277, 1992; ZYLBERSTEIN, J.-Cl., BARENBOOM, A., *Traité de Maastricht, Mode d'emploi précédé de commentaires sur le Traité de Maastricht et suivi du traité de Rome*, Paris XIII, U.G.E., 10/18, s.d.

For purposes of facility I will use here the term EC law to refer to Community law, including the Treaty on the European Union.

4 The argument is that if a worker is offered a job in a Member-State of the Union, his family should be allowed to join, or to follow him or her, only in as far as the very fact of not being allowed to do so would weigh on the worker's decision to take the job, and - eventually - make him or her decide not to take that job. Family life thus 'endangers' free circulation of labour - and therefore it should be protected.

5 Council Directive 90/364 on the right of residence, Council Directive on the right of residence for employees and self-employed persons who have ceased their occupational activity 90/365, Official Journal of the European Community, 1990 L 180/26;28 and 30 and Council Directive 93/96 on the right of residence for students, ibid., 1993, C 317/93, 59 ff. For commentary on these directives, see i.a.: O'KEEFFE, 'The Free Movement of Persons and the Single Market', *European Law Review*, 1992, no1, p. 3-19: VAN NUFFEL, P., 'Een bijna algemeen verblijfsrecht in de Europese Gemeenschap. Commentaar op de verblijfsrechtrichtlijnen van 28 juni 1990', Sociaal economische wetgeving. *Tijdschrift voor Europees en economisch recht*, 1990, no12, p. 887 ff.

6 ibid.

7 The right to freely move within the territories of the Member-States sets in motion extensive human mobility. It has i.a. multiplied the relatively massive fluxes of pensioners from Germany, The Netherlands, Luxemburg and Belgium who, each winter, leave their country for no other purposes than enjoying for several months the mild climate in Spain and Portugal.

8 'Directives' are compulsory to the Member-States, but they require transposition in national law.

9 See i.a.: WEILER, J.H.H., 'The Transformation of Europe', Yale Law Journal, 1992, p. 2403-2483.

10 Cf. supra note 5.

11 See on this point: Commission of the EC, 'The Role of Education and Training in the Completion of the Internal Market', *Social Europe*, 1988, p. 36 ff.; FLYNN, J., 'Vocational Training in Community Law and Practice', *Yearbook of European Law*, 1989, p. 59-85.

12 This principle of non-discrimination causes serious financial problems for some universities in Member-States that did not - or not yet - introduce a numerus clausus system: they have to enroll students from other countries who failed or are afraid of not passing the numerus clausus in the home country. Some faculties of medicine in Belgium for the moment count more German and Dutch students than Belgian students. See i.a.: GILLIAMS, H., 'Van Gravier tot Erasmus: over de bijdrage van het Hof van Justitie tot de uitbouw van een Europees onderwijsbeleid', *Rechtskundig Weekblad*, 1989-1990, p. 494-504.

13 Cf. supra note 5.

14 See i.a.: HOOGENBOOM, T., 'Free Movement of non-EC nationals, Schengen and Beyond', in: MEYERS, H. e.a. (eds;), *Schengen. Internationalisation of Central Chapters of the Law on Aliens, Refuges, Security and the Police*, Zwolle, Tjeenk-Willink/Kluwer Law and Taxation, 1991, p. 83 ff.; SCHERMERS, H.G. (ed.), *Free Movement of Persons in Europe. Legal Problems and Experiences*, The Hague, T.M.C. Asser Institute, 1993.

15 cf. infra note 16.
16 Article 3 EEC-Treaty states that 'the activities of the Community shall include [...] (c) the abolition, as between Member-States, of obstacles to freedom and movement for persons'.
17 On these treaties, see i.a.: Etude comparative des conditions et procédures d'introduction et d'accès à l'emploi de travailleurs des pays-tiers dans les états membres de la C.E., Brussels (Commission des Communautés européennes), 1982.
18 Namely the 1963 Association Agreement concluded with Turkey and its implementation (on this implementation, see i.a.: DE MOFFARTS, G., 'La libre circulation des travailleurs de nationalité turque et des membres de leur famille', Revue du droit des étrangers, 1985, n_33, p. 50 ff.), the 1975 Lomé Convention and the 1976 Cooperation Agreement with Morocco. And more recently, several Association Agreements with previous Eastern European countries.
19 Case 267/83, Diatta v. Land Berlin [1985], ECR 574.
20 Namely Article 10 of Regulation 1612/68. Article 10 is worded as follows:
1. The following shall, irrespective of their nationality, have the right to install themselves with a worker who is national of one Member-State and who is employed in the territory of another Member-State:
(a) his spouse and their descendants who are under the age of 21 years or are dependents;
(b) dependent relatives in the ascending line of the worker and his spouse.
2. Member-States shall facilitate the admission of any member of the family not coming within the provisions of paragraph 1 if dependent on the worker referred to above or living under his roof in the country whence he comes.
21 And even if they intend to divorce, as was the case in Diatta (cf. supra note 19).
22 European Commission, Family Reunification in the light of international law, Community law and/or practice, 13.05.92, V/384/92, p. 41-42.
23 For the purposes of the illustration, as I already mentioned, I do not take into account here Fatiha's own feelings and emotions. My argument deals with EC law rationale.
24 Cf. supra note 5.
25 Cf. supra note 20.
26 Conforming to the Court's interpretation in the Diatta case. Cf. supra 19.
27 Cf. supra note 5.
28 On these regulations, cf. supra note 1.
29 Cf. supra note 1.
30 On the European 'Resolution on Harmonization of Family Reunification', adopted in Copenhagen in 1993, see i.a.: BOELES, P., e.a., *A New Immigration Law for Europe?*, Utrecht, Nederlands Centrum Buitenlanders, 1993.
31 Which national legislations in the Member-States had to comply with by 1 January 1995.
32 In application of article 10, 4 of the Law of 15 December, 1980 that regulates the entry, the residence and the expulsion of foreigners from Belgium (Moniteur belge, 12 July, 1984).
33 The Reed case, for instance (Case 59/85, Judgment of 17 April, 1986) concerned the refusal of the Dutch authorities to issue a residence permit for a British woman, who cohabited with another, equally unmarried British woman who was employed in The Netherlands. The ECJ has stated that Ms. Reed did not enjoy the rights as a family member under EC provisions since she was not a migrant's worker 'spouse' .On the protection under EC law of family reunification with homosexual partners, see i.a.: JESSURUN d'OLIVEIRA, H.U., 'Lesbians and Gays and the Freedom of Movement of Persons', in: WAALDIJK, K., CLAPHAM, A. (eds), *Homosexuality: A European Community Issue* (Essays on Lesbian and Gay Rights in European Law and Policy), Dordrecht/Boston, M. Nijhoff Publishers, 1993, p. 289-316.
34 Love relations of course, are not solely relations between fiancés or spouses. Children may wish to have their parents come over and live with them in Europe. Many children are sending money to their parents abroad. Once they get the nationality of the host country, family reunification will be relatively easily granted to them. But as long as they remain TCNs reunifica-

tion will be extremely difficult: most immigration laws prohibit reunification between TCNs and relatives that are not either their children or their own wife or husband. Parents are not included in the group of 'authorized' relatives.

35 Which in turn, favours so-called fraudulous marriages: people are marrying preferably EC nationals that satisfy all conditions to enjoy the right to family reunification.

36 See i.a.: KEDZIA, Z., KORULA, A. & NOWAK, M. (eds), *Perspectives on an All-European System of Human Rights Protection. The Role of the Council of Europe, the CSCE and the European Communities* (Proceedings and Reçommendations of an International Conference), Poznan, Poland, 8-11 October 1990, Kehl, NP. Engel Verlag, 1991. Article F of the Treaty on the Union (1992) states explicitly that the Member States are determined to work together to promote democracy (F.1) and the fundamental rights recognized in the Convention for the Protection of Human Rights and Fundamental Freedoms (F.2).

37 See on this point, in relation to the protection of family ties, i.a.: WEILER, J.H.H., 'Thou shalt not oppress a stranger (Ex. 23:9). On the Judicial Protection of the Human Rights of Non-EC Nationals', in: SCHERMERS, H.G. (ed.), o.c., 1993, p. 248-271.

38 Except in the case of collective expulsion (Article 4 of the Fourth Protocol).

39 Article 8 of the treaty provides for the right to respect for anyone's private and family life, his home and his correspondence, in a quasi-unlimited way, of all persons living on the territory of the Member-States to the Convention. The only restriction to the protection of that right being the possibility for a public authority to interfere in case the 'interests of national security, public safety or the economic well-being of the country is involved, for prevention of disorder or crime, for the protection of health and morals, or for the protection of the rights and freedoms of others'.

40 Case of Abdulaziz, Cabales & Balkandali, judgment of 28 May, 1985, series A no. 94, p. 34 ff.

41 However, when it was established that under similar circumstances a wife would be permitted to enter the United Kingdom in order to join her husband, the Court found an infringement of Article 14 which prohibits discrimination, inter alia, on the basis of sex.

42 Moustaquim case, judgment of 18 February, 1991, Series A, no 193.

43 This is evidenced in the Treaty on the European Union of 1992 that reaffirms the decision of the Member-States to promote democracy based on the fundamental rights that are acknowledged in the Member-States and in the Human Rights Treaties.

Notes on Fassbinder's "Angst essen Seele auf"[1]

THOMAS SPIJKERBOER

As will be clear from most other contributions to this collection of essays, lawyers tend to think of a theme such as Love and Law as a theme of legal theory. Migration lawyers however know that love is at the heart of much of everyday legal practice, because love and residence rights have a lot to do with each other. Marie-Claire Foblet's article is an expression of that knowledge. In this essay, I want to explore the politics of migration, love and law. This exploration will follow in the footsteps of *Angst essen Seele auf* (Fear eat Soul), a film directed by Rainer Werner Fassbinder that was released in 1974. Because my analysis comes out of the film, I will first tell you the story.

The film is about the love affair between an older German woman, Emmi, and a young Moroccan guest worker whose name is Salem, but who is called Ali by all. Emmi goes into a cafe in order to shelter from the rain. The cafe, which is frequented only by guest workers, is run by two bartenders/prostitutes, Katharina and Barbara. When Salem does not agree to Katharina's suggestion that they go to her room together, she asks him if, then, he wants to dance with the old woman. Salem invites Emmi for a dance, and after the dance they have a drink together and talk. Salem escorts Emmi home, and Emmi invites Salem in because it is still raining. They talk. Emmi is a lonely widow doing cleaning jobs. Salem is a guest worker, living in squalid housing. Salem misses the last streetcar and he stays for the night. They end up spending the night together. The next morning they part, and at work Emmi discusses guest workers with her colleagues. The colleagues have lots of racist remarks to make, and are horrified of German women who have relationships with guest workers. Visiting her daughter Krista and her husband Eugen, Emmi tells them she has fallen in love with a Moroccan man twenty years her junior. The children react in disbelief, and Eugen remarks to Krista that her mother is beginning to become demented. Emmi then goes looking for Salem in the cafe, but doesn't find him. When she returns home, he is waiting for her on the street.

They start living together. One night, the son of the landlord, Mr. Gruber, comes by. He is very polite, but says that sub-letting is forbidden and therefore Salem will have to leave. Emmi says that Salem is not a tenant but her future husband. In that case, Mr. Gruber does not see a problem. When Emmi explains to Salem that she got rid of Gruber by telling him that they were going to marry, Salem finds marrying a great idea. They celebrate their engagement in the cafe with Salem's friends; they dance. The marriage itself is celebrated by just the two of them in a very expensive restaurant. The waiter seizes every opportunity to use French or English terms that Emmi doesn't know, stares at them and seems to be only just willing to serve them.

When other people hear of the marriage, they turn their backs. Emmi has invited her three children to her home in order to tell them of her marriage and to present Salem. When he enters, Bruno kicks in the TV and leaves; Albert calls his mother a whore and follows Bruno; and Krista announces that Eugen and she don't want to stay in this pig sty. The shopkeeper where Emmi has done her shopping for decades refuses to serve Salem, and when Emmi protests he also refuses to serve Emmi. The neighbours, who have been following the goings on with increasing abhorrence, tell Emmi to clean better because the staircase is so dirty these days, and do many more of these kind of tiny nasty things. And Emmi's colleagues completely ignore her, for example not noticing when Emmi asks them to pass her the knife during lunch. When Salem asks his friends from the cafe over to Emmi's house and they all play Ludo, the neighbours call the police. Two very kind policemen politely suggest to Emmi to turn down the music, not because it is particularly loud but because the neighbours complain. Emmi can't stand it any more and breaks down. Salem and Emmi decide to go on holiday. Emmi fantasises that when they return, everybody will be nice to them.

And that is what happens. The shopkeeper gets a lot of competition from the new supermarket next door, and almost forces Emmi in for a nice chat. The neighbours ask Emmi if they can borrow part of her cellar which she does not use, and when Emmi offers that Salem will carry some heavy things for them, they are delighted. At Emmi's work, one colleague has been dismissed because of petty theft, and they discuss strategies to get a pay rise. In this, the new colleague, a Yugoslav woman, is ignored in the same way Emmi was ignored earlier. And Bruno asks Emmi to baby sit his daughter so that his wife can start work. He has already sent a cheque for the TV.

Emmi not only orders Salem to carry the things for the neighbours, but generally starts to tell him what to do, wear, eat, like. When Salem wants cous-cous, she says that he should adapt to the German way of life. She shows him off to her colleagues, who touch him admiringly. Salem visits Barbara twice, where he has sex and cous-cous. When he doesn't return to Emmi's house at night, Emmi goes to look for him at his work, a garage. Neither Salem nor his colleagues directly acknowledge her presence. One of the colleagues asks Salem if this is his granny from Morocco.

The semi-final scene first shows Salem at the cafe, drinking a lot, gambling, and losing lots of money. Emmi enters, and sits down at the table where she sat in the first scene. She asks Barbara to put on the record they danced to, 'Hey black gypsy, come, play something for me'. Salem asks Emmi for a dance. They make up: Salem says he doesn't want other women but only wants Emmi; Emmi says she understands his desire for younger women. They want to stick together, together they are strong. Suddenly Salem collapses. In the hospital, next to the bed where Salem lies sleeping, the doctor explains to Emmi that Salem has a typical guest workers' illness: an ulcer. He will recover, but get another ulcer in half a year. Emmi says that that won't happen, because she will do whatever she can. The doctor wishes her good luck and leaves. The last image shows Emmi holding Salem's hand.

Salem's body

The first thing Salem says refers to his body. Explaining to Katharina why he won't come with her, he says 'Dick broken' (55).[2] In the final scene in the hospital, Salem's entire body is broken in a way that, as the doctor explains, is typical for guest workers. Salem's body is fundamentally deficient, both sexually and as a body that can work.

Salem's body is eroticized. When Salem and Emmi meet, Salem dresses in a dark suit. During their first meeting, Emmi says to Salem that he should wear bright clothes, because dark things look so sad (58). He then begins to wear tight T-shirts, which emphasise his biceps and pectorals, and tight blue jeans that show a bulge in his crotch and highlight his round ass. Later, Salem's body is displayed for Emmi's colleagues. On Emmi's invitation, they touch his biceps and one of them appreciatingly comments 'Terrific. And the skin is so soft' (91). Salem's body is the one we see naked several times. When Emmi awakes after their first night together, Emmi is dressed but we see Salem naked from his waist on; when, the evening before, he comes into Emmi's room the coat of his pyjama is unbuttoned. He walks around in Emmi's house in briefs and an unbuttoned dressing gown.

We see Salem's body entirely naked in two key scenes. After the marriage, but before the holiday, Salem takes a shower after work. Via the mirror, we see his body. Emmi walks into the bathroom, and also via the mirror looks at him. Salem returns the look. Emmi says 'You are very beautiful.' Salem laughs (77). Salem's body is admired and commented on by Emmi, in a way in which female bodies can be treated. It is unmasculine to have the passive role of the erotic spectacle, of an object. Silverman characterizes Salem's smile as one 'with the modesty of someone whose pleasure in himself is entirely dependent upon the pleasure another takes in him' (Silverman 1992, 140). This role of erotic spectacle, that can be put on display at the wishes of someone else (as in the scene with Emmi's colleagues), emasculates Salem. In Freudian vocabulary, it de-phallicises him -- in other words, it breaks his dick.

The other scene in which we see Salem naked is when Salem visits Barbara's home for the second time. Salem undresses. In the sex scene that follows, we would expect Salem to be a libidinous black man, a kind of sexual magician, as in western culture black men are eroticized as powerful and sexy bodies. But we see the reverse. In Barbara's home, Salem's body constantly is weak: his hands dangle next to his body, his head droops. When they have sex, Salem lies on top of Barbara, but he lies completely still. The thing that moves is not his penis but her arm caressing him.

In this way, Fassbinder argues that Salem's eroticization emasculates him. He can be eroticized and made into a spectacular object because he is the least powerful character in the film. Bell hooks, among others, has argued that in white culture, black men cannot be 'real men' because they cannot assume proper patriarchal functions, i.e. assert legitimate domination over women. The idea that black men are sex freaks is caused by the idea that, as they cannot be real men in patriarchal terms, they must shift their masculinity to the other source of masculinity: phallocentrism. That is why black dicks necessarily must be bigger; black men's masculinity depends entirely on their sexual prowess (hooks 1992, 87-113). Fassbinder makes this white mythology of the black sexual maniac present, but he denies it. Salem is impotent. He can't compensate for his emasculation by having sex. Sexuality is not a realm separate from power relations, but it is one of the realms where power is constituted and expressed.

Apart from being sexy, Salem's body can work. A first thing to be remarked is Salem's gallantry. He not only invites Emmi for a dance. He also helps her into her coat, keeps doors open for her, carries bags, holds up umbrellas, etc. But because of what takes place between Salem and Emmi, this gallantry more and more becomes subservience, work carried out on Emmi's orders.

Salem works at a garage. There, he says, Germans and Arabs are not equal: 'German master,[3] Arab dog'. Emmi is indignant about this, but Salem says it is best not to think about it (56). But Emmi in her turn will use Salem as labour. She tells him to help the neighbour move her things after the holiday, and ends her order with 'Understood?', to which Salem replies 'Understand' (85) -- an exchange that is more typical of the relationship between boss and worker than between wife and husband.

Although of course it is very manly that Salem can carry all kinds of things, it is unmanly that he does so at the orders of his wife. This parallels the eroticization of his body. At the garage where he works, he also performs a masculine job. But he has the role of a dog vis-à-vis his boss, and the work and work relationships make him (and other guest workers) ill, as we see at the end of the film. Salem's body can be eroticized and it can work. He can be appreciated as a body. But the appreciation has as its condition and price his emasculation. Sex and work are the areas where Salem is appreciated in the role of the powerless.

Emmi's body

During the first scene, Emmi is referred to as 'the old one' by Barbara and Katharina (54-55). In the last scene but one, Emmi says she understands Salem's unfaithfulness because she knows how old she is (95). Salem is not a real man because he is black; Emmi is not a real woman because of her age.

During the first scenes, Emmi does not look beautiful. Her hair is a mess and she doesn't use make-up. When Emmi gets out of bed after her first night with Salem, at first she is not aware that he is in her bed. She turns around, discovers him, and rushes to the bathroom in panic. She looks at herself in the mirror. Then Salem is standing in the bathroom door and says hello. With tears in her eyes, she turns to him and they embrace. From that moment on, she starts doing her hair, probably dying it, putting lipstick on, dressing better. But her looks in no way resemble the amazing dress and make-up of Barbara, who has glittering dresses with deep cleavages, exuberant lipstick and eye shadow. Emmi is not a spectacle because she is too old for that. The camera never desires her; we only see her entirely dressed, the stills of her are stills of an old woman while those of Salem often show a sexy Arab. She can be desired, which comes as a pleasant surprise to her, but only by a man who is characterized by lack. Emmi's femininity has been seriously damaged. She is not a virgin, she has been married before, and she can't have children any more. Therefore, she will have to do with a surrogate man and won't get beyond a fake femininity. To the outside world, the fact that she enjoys Salem's advances does not show that she is desirable, but that she is a whore, as her children, her colleagues and Katharina and Barbara say.

Emmi says that work is half of life (56). She works as a cleaning woman, but initially she doesn't dare to say that because she is ashamed of it. Cleaning women are rare these days, she says. She never learnt something proper (57). Her work accentuates her status as an older woman.

Here, as with Salem's body, the camera sees Emmi's body as dominant ideology sees her. She is not a real woman, and therefore the only explanation for the fact that Salem desires her is his own undesirability. The viewer is given the perspective of 'normality': older women are not sexy, non-white men are only sexy if they are objects, a relation between an older white woman and a young non-white man is impossible. But the film shows the devastating effects of this 'normality', and as we will see ends destabilizing it. Giving the spectator the normative perspective of 'normality' turns out not to be a way in which we are made to accept it. Quite the contrary: we are confronted with how we look.

The name

Salem calls himself Ali when he meets Emmi. Emmi replies by saying 'You're called Ali?' (56), and Salem says:

SALEM Not Ali. But all say Ali. Now I am Ali.
EMMI But what is your name really?
SALEM El Hedi ben Salem M'Barek Mohammed Mustafa.
EMMI Oh - it is very long, this name.
SALEM Yes. Everything in Tismit[4] has a long name. (57)

Emmi calls Salem by the name of Ali during the entire film. Thus, she calls him by the name that he has according to Germans who find his real name too complicated. The name here is not something of the surface; it is what Salem is ('Now I am Ali'). Salem does not try to give Emmi access to some real, authentic self, nor does he want her to try. He only can present himself to Emmi as what he is in German society. He can only be a *Gastarbeiter*, and in a way Ali is his 'real' name.[5] For this reason, it is significant that Salem's 'real' name is mentioned twice in the movie. Once in the scene just quoted, and once when Emmi presents Salem to her children as her husband with the words 'So! That is my husband. El Hedi ben Salem M'Barek Mohammed Mustafa. I call him Ali.' (73) Here Emmi, like Salem earlier, says that Salem has a name; and that she calls him by a different one. This distinction is made at the two moments Salem is presented: once by himself to Emmi, and once by Emmi to her children. Salem's incomprehensible name is something for the record.[6]

The name Ali is a stereotypical one. At that, it is incorrect. Ali is, by my best knowledge, a common Turkish name, and not a common Moroccan name - certainly not among the Berbers like Salem (60). Yet Salem uses it for himself. One may consider this as the internalization of racism; but I think something more complex is at work. Salem can only live under his long and incomprehensible name in the surroundings where everything has a long name -- in his home town. In Germany, that complex thing is out of reach, not only for Emmi but also for himself. Fassbinder here explores an issue that he re-examined in later films: identity is not something real covered under surfaces, but it is inaccessible (and therefore in a way non-existent) if the surfaces don't allow for it. The identity of Ali is not any less real than Salem's.

Emmi also has two names. She is Mrs Kurowski -- which is the name of her deceased husband.[7] This name (we never learn about her maiden name) indicates her foreign connections, as one of the neighbours remarks when she has for the first time 'caught' Emmi with Salem on the stairs of her house. 'But that one isn't a proper German herself. Kurowski -- who has a name like that?' (59)

After marrying Salem, Emmi only once refers to herself by Salem's name, immediately after leaving the city hall.

EMMI Do you know what my name is now?
SALEM You long name.
EMMI Very long name. Emanuela ben Salem M'Barek Mohammed Mustafa. Sounds funny, no?
SALEM Much beautiful.
EMMI Well - beautiful? I don't know really.
SALEM Yes. Beautiful.
EMMI If you think so. (71)

Yet Emmi will remain Mrs Kurowski to everyone in the film, even though formally she has the funny name. She even doesn't really agree that it is beautiful. This situation is, let us say, offensive to Salem in two ways. First, she doesn't find his name beautiful; with the last words just quoted she laconically dismisses his other, Moroccan identity. But what is more, the fact that she does not bear his name shows a lack, or an impossibility or even impotence on Salem's side. 'Normally', when a woman marries a man she becomes his, and this is symbolized by her new name. Salem cannot do that, he can't posses her because he is emasculated. But, reversely, as we saw, Emmi is not a woman to be possessed. She has been possessed before, therefore is not a virgin, and she can't have children anymore. She has already made the journey from her father's name to the name of her husband. This is something that can be done to her only once. This is the more logical because Salem's German self, Ali, does not have a family name, so there is nothing Emmi can take on, there is no way for him to possess her, just as there is nothing to be possessed.

Inclusion and exclusion

When Emmi enters the cafe for the first time, the people in the cafe, who all stand at the counter, stare at her. She sits down with her back to the door, facing the people at the bar, and gives them intimidated looks. When Barbara goes to her to ask what she wants to have, her first words are 'Excuse me, but (..)' and she starts to explain that it rains outside (54). Emmi is excluded by the people in the cafe, and doesn't know how to react. Salem breaks through her isolation, and invites her for a dance. When they sit down afterwards, Emmi takes the chair that faces the door, with her back to the bar, while Salem sits with his face to the wall. In this way they defy Emmi's exclusion, not by confronting it or by trying to let her be part of the group, but by just doing what they like and in a way ignoring the others.

When, later that night, Emmi and Salem walk up the stairs, a neighbour who is constantly spying on the goings on in the staircase returns Emmi's money she lent, and stares at Salem through a grid that separates her part of the landing from the communal part. The stare is cold and hostile, and when Salem and Emmi have gone up she immediately goes to a neighbour who lives on the same landing, and they discuss what it is that Mrs Kurowski (who herself is 'not a proper German') is doing with a black man at 9.30 pm (59). This is the first sign that Emmi and Salem will both be excluded, Salem because he is black and Emmi because she is with Salem.

The next day, Emmi discusses guest workers and relationships between German women and guest workers with her colleagues. The words of her colleagues are an explicit announcement to her of what will happen if she carries on with Salem. Guest workers are just keen on money and think of women all the time. They are lazy swines who live at our expense. Women who have a relationship with guest workers are dirty whores who only think of sex, and they are completely ignored by their fellow Germans (63-64). When she tells Krista and Eugen that she is in love with a Moroccan who is twenty years younger, she is ridiculed (66-67).

When she goes to the cafe again in order to look for Salem after their first meeting, Barbara is the only other person there. She treats her coldly, and explicitly excludes her by saying 'By the way...the cafe belongs to me' (67).

When the son of the landlord comes and tells Emmi that Salem has to leave because subletting is contractually forbidden, the exclusion does not refer to Salem's ethnicity. In fact, Gruber behaves nicely because unlike the others he at least acknowledges Salem's presence, and says cheers to him when he has his brandy. Emmi, faced with this exclusion, makes a smart move. She says that they are going to marry. The contract does not prohibit marriage, nor does it prohibit spouses living together. Although he expresses his surprise, Gruber reacts amazingly liberally. And he does not say Emmi is an old whore, as many others will, but says 'You are old enough to know what you do' (69) and leaves. Marriage is such a mainstream thing that, it seems at first, it is impossible to exclude you once you have married.

But at the restaurant where they celebrate their marriage, they are made to feel utterly out of place. The waiter uses another strategy of exclusion. He doesn't miss a single opportunity to make Emmi aware that she doesn't know how to behave, she doesn't know what certain words or expressions mean, and stares at her. The exclusionary technique here is not ethnicity, age or gender, but class.

When Emmi announces her marriage to her children and presents Salem, they call her a whore, her house a pig sty, and break off all relations. The shopkeeper also refuses to deal with both Salem and Emmi, as do the neighbours and Emmi's colleagues. The night that Salem invites some friends from the cafe to their home, Katharina refuses to go to the home of 'the old whore' (79). In the last scene before the holiday, Salem and Emmi are sitting together, isolated in a huge space. People just stare, and don't react to Emmi's protests against their behaviour. The last argument she has is their respectability: 'He is my husband. My Husband' (83).

After the holiday, the exclusion of Emmi and Salem is over suddenly. The shopkeeper discovers it is against his business interests to scare clients away; the neighbours discover the material advantages of good neighbourly relations and of a man who can carry things around; the most brutal son (the guy who kicked the TV in) needs Emmi as a baby-sitter; her colleagues need Emmi's solidarity in their schemes for a higher salary and enjoy Salem's sex appeal. But then it turns out that by being included, Emmi and Salem become a part of the group of people that excludes. Emmi is co-opted by her colleagues into excluding the new Yugoslav colleague and the former colleague who committed some petty crime. Emmi seizes the opportunity to make the relationship with Salem into a hierarchical one, ordering him to do odd jobs, telling him what to wear, showing him off to her colleagues, and summoning him to stop whining about cous-cous and to integrate. Then Salem wants to be alone and leaves. There is no room for him anymore -- he simply is not German. He reacts by seeing Barbara, so by setting up a relationship that excludes Emmi. Leaving is a powerless way to exclude Emmi, but nevertheless a way to hit her where it hurts. Emmi has become dependent on him for feeling like someone; she may have been a lonesome miser before, but now she at least has power over one person, who shouldn't extract himself from her power. When she goes to Salem's workplace to look for him, she is excluded from this all-male environment. No one reacts to what she does or says; she is made fun of. During their last dance, Emmi and Salem acknowledge their mutual dependence. But then what Emmi in a way wanted happens: he becomes totally dependent on her by falling ill, she has total power over him now. But the power is useless, because Salem lying unconscious in a hospital bed is so powerless that it is no use having power over him.[8]

It is clear that the initial external rejection of Salem and Emmi is the glue to their relationship, and that when this glue vanishes the cracks begin to show. But small details in the scenes before the holiday make clear that the cracks were there all along. Emmi doesn't know how to deal with, and in many ways rejects Salem's being Moroccan. Salem can't cope with his emasculation which is illustrated by the fact that he 'only' can get Emmi (an old whore) or Barbara (a young whore).

During the final dance however there is a beginning of something substantially different. Emmi speaks of her comprehension for Salem's desire for a younger woman and says that that is not what really counts. She doesn't want to forbid him things, which is at least a partial renunciation of her hierarchically superior position. Salem chooses for her, and says he is so nervous, which is a beginning admission of the fact that he has some problems. This would have been romantic, but turns into melodrama when Salem falls down because of his guest workers' illness. Their last lines are statements on their communality. They are both in a weak position, but 'Together we are strong' (95). That is true in one way, and not in another one, as the next scene shows. But in the hospital, Emmi promises to stand by Salem. This a rather ambiguous ending, maybe on purpose. The viewer is left with the question: is this a happy ending or not? There were hints of something different, but can it hold? What were the problems facing Emmi and Salem, and have they begun to solve them?

The law

The law takes on three different forms in this film. The first, marriage, is the apparition of law that we all aspire to. The second one, the tenancy agreement, represents its contractual form ('we agreed to this'). The third form, the police, stands for its repressive version.

Emmi first mentions marriage when she explains to the landlord that Salem is not subletting a room in her apartment (which is forbidden by the rent contract), but is going to be her husband. When she explains this to Salem, he finds marriage a good idea, and so they marry. The marriage is thus a strategy in order to stave off the condemning reaction of the outside world. Emmi and Salem try to gain respectability for their ethnically and generationally mixed, and therefore unacceptable relationship. They don't succeed in becoming respectable, however. In the restaurant where they celebrate their marriage, they are almost ignored, and are made to feel that they don't know how they should behave in such surroundings. The announcement of their marriage to Emmi's children has dramatic results: Bruno kicks in the TV, Albert says it's a shame and calls his mother a whore, and Krista calls her mother's house a pig sty. The shopkeeper, the neighbours and Emmi's colleagues all stick to their positions. When, after the holiday, people miraculously drop their racism, it is not because of the marriage but because Salem to them is a useful body.

One would almost say that the marriage doesn't make any difference, but that is too soon a conclusion. After the holiday, a neighbour refers to Salem as Emmi's husband (86) when he is carrying furniture. One of the main themes of the film, that Salem is only accepted on the terms of the surroundings, i.e. as a body, is relevant to the marriage as well. Emmi and Salem can only conceive of their relationship as proper in terms of marriage. They buy respectability by buying into a patriarchal institution. But they cannot dispose of this institution at will; it would be more appropriate to say that the institution disposes of them. Marriage does not allow for their non-standard relationship. Salem cannot be to Emmi what a proper man is to his woman, who is not a proper woman either. This may be fine, as long as their relationship is not defined, as at the beginning of the film. When it is defined, the specificity of their relationship becomes a lack because neither of them is a proper member of her/his sex. Therefore, Salem has to look for what is missing (sex, cous-cous and alcohol) elsewhere. In this way, marriage makes a lot of difference. Because their relationship is impossible as a marriage, it is impossible in marriage. Marriage tears Emmi and Salem apart.

The tenancy contract is one of the things that forces Emmi and Salem to conform, by marrying in order to evade the prohibition of subletting. Gruber displays no racism whatsoever--he even says good night to Salem (69). At first, he points out that subletting is forbidden by the contract. In this way, he no doubt acts as an agent of the other tenants. But he is polite, and when Emmi does some window-dressing ('we will marry') he admits that that is something completely different. He is, however, the external force that brings Emmi and Salem to marry; he is a force of conformity. When, later, the other tenants ask him if he can't do something about this rabble (Emmi and Salem), he says he can't discover anything improper (82). Gruber has never been racist, but he illustrates the futility of just not being biased. He is part of the system nevertheless -- and, of course, collects the rent.[9]

The police is the third form of the law, and represents its repressive aspect. The policemen are called by the neighbours who complain about the noise that Emmi, Salem and his friends make when they play Ludo. But, as one of the neighbours remarks in shock, the police officers have long hair. In fact, they behave extremely nice. They say to Emmi they're sorry, but the neighbours complain.... They leave immediately. Emmi says: 'They've set the police on our neck' (80-81). This is the velvet glove. The police might do worse things; that is the threat Emmi immediately feels. They don't, but they still convey the threat. They also, politely and all, convey the racism of the neighbours. The fact that they seem to realise this, and make excuses, does not make that any different. Like the landlord, the police can afford not being racist at all.

Fassbinder here portrays the law not as a purely repressive force, although he makes one reference to the threat of physical violence. In the context of its time, it was rather polemical to portray policemen as basically decent people. It was more commonplace on the German left to depict them as pigs who enjoyed beating up the proletariat. But in this film, law mainly has its power effects because people aspire to it, see themselves as part of it, and find it a respectable thing. Law is depicted as an ideological phenomenon more than as a source of repression in the literal sense. The power of law comes from its effect on people's minds, from the fact that people are willing to conform to, and even to long for the oppressive community standards that it embodies.

The politics of love and law

Fassbinder has been criticized vehemently because, according to his critics, he depicted a world of oppression without possibilities of resistance.[10] The critics would have preferred Fassbinder to show the oppressed of the world the way out. This can be illustrated by how Fassbinder represents economic exploitation. In tune with the leftist rhetoric of the period, Salem and Emmi are represented as exploited workers. But Fassbinder's analysis doesn't end there, because these exploited workers are not innocent. Emmi exploits Salem's labour power, and at her work she joins in excluding the new Yugoslav colleague. In the scene at Salem's work, Salem is part of a male world that excludes Emmi, and he hires a prostitute in order to exclude Emmi. Economic exploitation, like other forms of exclusion, has many sources, and there is no outside of this system. There is no clearly definable class or group of people, such as the proletariat, the intelligentsia, or the revolutionary avant-garde, that can carry the banner forward. Richard Dyer, elaborating on the 'reactionary implications' of Fassbinder's films, finds him guilty of 'left-wing melancholy', which is a view of life that 'recognises the exploitativeness of capitalist society but is unable to see any means by which fundamental change in this society can take place. (...) it does not see the working class as the agent of historical change' (Dyer 1979, 55).[11] Fassbinder's critics presumed that for radical politics it is required that there is one unpolluted entity which can be the source of unalienated political action.

Fassbinder's political activism is located precisely within this claustrophobic setting. He analyzes the processes of exclusion, oppression and alienation, and emphatically denies that one can withdraw from them. But in the world he creates, that analysis is not the end but a beginning. This becomes clear from the role of dance in this film.

There is one way out for the bodies of Emmi and Salem, that are represented in a way that seems to be despairing. At the beginning, in the middle and at the end, they dance to the tune of 'Hey black gypsy, come, play something for me', sung by a Zarah Leander-like voice (55, 70, 95). There can hardly be any doubt that Salem is the black gypsy, and Emmi the me. This song title doesn't deny who's who. But it is the occasion for the meeting, the celebration of the decision to marry, and the reconciliation, for the first and the last conversation, and for being together unconditionally. These moments of genuine contact occur in a marginal place: the guest worker's cafe and/or brothel. As most notably Salem's ulcer attack makes clear, the margin is not a safe refuge. But dancing is an act of defiance. Moving, intently and carefully, aware of each other's shortcomings (Emmi can't dance, and Salem clearly also doesn't know how to really), and this to a tune that is the articulation of white woman's racialized longing for an exotic male -- this is not a safe refuge but a small mutiny. Dance, here as in many other Fassbinder films, is an intimate act that is dependent on and sensitive to (in the terms of the period) 'the objective circumstances', that makes a difference not despite those circumstances, but because it takes them on and thereby transforms them.

Fassbinder analyzes, in Foucault's term, the micro-physics of power. Fassbinder wrote that he thought that love is the best, sneakiest and most effective instrument of social oppression (quoted in Fassbinder 1990, 184). But this does not only show how omnipresent power is. It also shows how many possible points of resistance there are. And what is more: it reveals that people are actually using them. The identities and subject position for which the law recruits us are not simply lies, because in a very physical way they are truths to us. 'Positive thinking' does not efface the emasculation of migrant men; it does not do away with the reduction of women to their reproductive and sexual function. Praise of multiculturalism does not help against the clashes that bicultural relationships lead to -- both with the external world and between the partners involved. It is more productive not to deny the reality of law's power, and to grasp the glimpses of transformation that we can get by seeing and enjoying the resistance that people put up in their mundane everyday lives.This does not mean however that Fassbinder abdicated from politics in a broader sense and only opted for politics at a marginal micro level. But the dance of Emmi and Salem is where it all begins. As Fassbinder said about *Angst essen Seele auf*:

> *I want to show now how you can resist and can make it somehow nevertheless. Today I tend to believe that when you just reproduce these depressing circumstances, you reinforce them. That is why you should make the existing circumstances transparant ('durchschaubar'), so that it becomes conscious that they can be overcome (Spaich 1992, 266).*

> *Yes, we wanted to try to keep it (the story, TS) so simple that people*

> *would keep thinking: All sorts of things would be possible. I don't consider human beings incapable of change. It's built into the structure of my film that people begin to see, Yes, it is better if things are a bit different. And if you think it out a little more, things can even be better. I'm not capable of providing a grand ideological scheme, and that's not my job, either; other people are better trained and equipped for that. What interests me are these little opportunities, because I know something about them and find them stimulating*
> *(Fassbinder 1992, 12).*

Notes:

1 This a revised version of a talk given at the seminar on Love and Law in Europe, organized by the Faculty of Law of the University of Copenhagen on 26-27 April 1996. I am very much indebted to Betty de Hart, who commented on an earlier draft of this text.

2 Page numbers refer to the script, published in Fassbinder 1990, 51-96. Quotes are my translation from German.

3 Salem here indeed uses the word *Herr*, from the Nazi vocabulary *Herrenvolk* etc.

4 Tismit is the village where Salem comes from, 56.

5 It is significant that the translations of the film's title stress the name. In English, the film was released as *Ali: Fear Eats the Soul*, in French as *Tous les autres s'apellent Ali* (All the others are called Ali). The film was released in the Netherlands at that time as *Alle Turken heten Ali* (All Turks are called Ali; Förster 1993, 38), but now foreign films are (re-)released under their foreign name in the Netherlands.

6 This gets some more sharpness when we remind ourselves that the actor playing Salem had the same complicated name in real life and was Fassbinder's lover at the moment the film was made.

7 Salem is a *Gastarbeiter*; Emmi's first husband was a *Fremdarbeiter*, which is the term (or name) used for young men from the countries occupied by Nazi Germany who were forced to work in German industries.

8 This ending is a close parallel to the ending of *Martha*, where a sadistic husband regains his total power over his masochistic wife when she has an accident and, in the final scene, sits in a wheelchair pushed around by him.

9 It seems that Fassbinder collected the rent from guest workers living in the squalid lodging houses of his father after he had been struck off the medical register, Hayman 1984, 13.

10 See e.g. Silverman 1992, 155.

11 Dyer later retracts a bit from this all-out attack on Fassbinder. He ows up that because Fassbinder is influential, he'd 'rather have Fassbinder on my side' (Dyer 1979, 60). He grants Fassbinder's films a certain 'effectivity', but this is 'an effectivity that cannot be automatically read off from the films themselves, an effectivity moreover that the films do not, as it were, deserve.' (ibid, 55). This kind of criticism is relevant to Fassbinder's films, because it represents precisely the kind of orthodoxy that he attacked.

References:

Richard Dyer (1979): Reading Fassbinder's Sexual Politics, in: Tony Ryans (ed): *Fassbinder*, second edition, British Film Institute, London, p. 54-64.

Rainer Werner Fassbinder (1990): *Fassbinders Filme* 3, herausgegeben von Micheal Töteberg, Verlag der Autoren, Frankfurt am Main.

Rainer Werner Fassbinder (1992): *The Anarchy of the Imagination.* Interviews, Essays, Notes, edited by Michael Töteberg and Leo A. Lensing, translated by Krishna Winston, John Hopkins University Press.

Annette Förster (1993): Bekend en gruwelijk. Fassbinder in retrospectief [Familiar and horrible. Fassbinder in retrospective], in: Annette Förster, Juliette Jansen, Henk Camping: *Fassbinder*, Filmtheater 't Hoogt, Utrecht.

Ronald Hayman (1984): *Fassbinder Filmmaker*, Simon and Schuster, New York.

bell hooks (1992): *Black Looks. Race and Representation*, South End Press, Boston MA.

Kaya Silverman (1992): *Male Subjectivity at the Margins*, Routledge, New York and London.

Herbert Spaich (1992): *Rainer Werner Fassbinder. Leben und Werk*, Beltz, Weinheim.

Hagbard and Signe. A Medieval Tale on Tragic Love. From the History of the Danes

SAXO GRAMMATICUS

There were once women in Denmark who dressed themselves to look like men and spent almost every minute cultivating soldiers' skills, they did not want the sinews of their valour to lose tautness and be infected by self-indulgence. Loathing a dainty style of living, they would harden body and mind with toil and endurance, rejecting the fickle pliancy of girls and compelling their womanish spirits to act with a virile ruthlessness. They courted military celebrity so earnestly that you would have guessed they had unsexed themselves. Those especially who had forceful personalities or were tall and elegant embarked on this way of life. As if they were forgetful of their true selves they put toughness before allure, aimed at conflicts instead of kisses, tasted blood, not lips, sought the clash of arms rather than the arm's embrace, fitted to weapons hands which should have been weaving, desired not the couch but the kill, and those they could have appeased with looks they attacked with lances. Now I shall return from this byway to my main narrative.

At the beginning of spring Alf and Alger resumed their pirating expeditions. They were navigating different parts of the ocean when they came with their hundred ships on Prince Hamund's sons Helvin, Hagbarth and Hamund. Battle was engaged and only as the darkness of twilight parted their blood-weary hands were the soldiers ordered to keep truce during the night. The next day this was confirmed for good by a mutual oath; so many injuries had been sustained on both sides in the precious day's fight that there was no possibility of combat being renewed. The participants were driven to make peace when equally-matched bravery had exhausted them.

During the same period Hildigisl, a man of noble Teuton family, requested the hand of Sigars's daughter Signe, confident in his handsomeness and rank. His insignificance brought out her utter contempt; to her he seemed spineless and to be building his fortunes on the worth of others. It was his proved reputation for mighty deeds that had specially turned her affections towards Haki. She had a higher regard for the valiant than the feeble and admired decorations for achievement more than a decorative face; all the charms of beauty, she knew, grow cheap when valued against sheer courage, for they cannot balance it in the scales. There are some girls who are fascinated more by a lover's prestige than his shape, who go by the features of the mind not the countenance and are kindled to exchange marriage-vows only by consideration of a man's spirits.

Now while Hagbarth was on his way to Denmark with Sigar's sons, unknown to them he managed to talk with their sister and eventually extracted from her a faithful promise to become his mistress secretly. Later, when her maids happened to be comparing the distinguished reputations of noblemen, she put Haki before Hildigisl, stating that the latter had nothing but his figure to recommend him, while the flourishing soul of Haki compensated for the blemish on his face. Nor was she content to elevate him with this straight-forward compliment, but is said to have sung the following song:

This man lacks charm, but shines in the forefront of excellence,
his features gauged by their forcefulness.
For a lofty spirit redeems a rough appearance
and overcomes physical defects.
His mien flashes with valour, a face helped
by fierceness, honoured for its rigour.
A stern judge of behaviour praises the visage
for the mind, not the mind for beauty.
Shapeliness does not enhance a man's value, but daring
and renown achieved with arms.
Only a fine head boosts the other, a glowing
countenance and lustrous locks.
Empty loveliness stales, the deceptive glory
of looks is its own ruin.
Elegance and valour are governed by different objectives;
one lasts, the other perishes.
Bloom alone brings corruption; beneath the slipping
years it gradually vanishes.
Manliness better strengthens the heart, for it does not
lapse and fall in a moment.
The people's esteem is duped by the outwardly fair,
misses the rule of right.
But my judgment gives stronger acclaim to fortitude,
spurning a graceful presence.

Her voice reached the bystanders' ears, but in such a way that they believed she was praising Hagbarth under the name of Haki. Since Hildigisl was upset to learn of her preference for Hagbarth over himself, he bribed Bolvis, a blind man, to induce the sons of Sigar and those of Hamund to change their fellowship to hatred. Bilvis and Bolvis were old men employed by Sigar to counsel him in nearly all his affairs. These two had quite contrasting characters; one used to reconcile quarrelling parties, while the other loved to divide close friends by sowing resentment between them and fan unhealthy jealousies into complete ruptures. First, then, Bolvis disparaged the sons of Sigar to Hamund's offspring with lies and slanders, maintaining that it was never their custom to observe oaths of brotherhood constantly and peaceably; they could not be held in check by a compact, only by force of arms. So the young men's alliance broke down and while Hagbarth was far away, Sigar's sons, Alf and Alger, sprang an assault on Helvin and Hamund and killed them at the harbour they call Hamund's bay. Afterwards, to avenge his brothers, Hagbarth fell upon them with fresh forces and crushed them in battle. Hildigisl had both buttocks pinned with a spear but got away. The incident provided an opportunity to have a good laugh at the Teutons, for the unseemly injury certainly branded him with disgrace.

Later on, as if he had not stricken Sigar's daughter enough with the slaying of her brothers, Hagbarth dressed himself in woman's clothing and went back alone to her, relying on the promise she had made him and feeling more secure in her loyalty than alarmed because of the deed he had done. This is the extent to which desire makes light of danger. To advance a plausible reason for his expedition he professed to be a fighting-woman of Haki's coming from him on embassy to Sigar. At night when he retired to bed among the maidservants, the slaves who were washing and towelling his feet asked why his legs were so hairy and his hands not very soft to the touch. He answered:

'What wonder if tender hollow of my foot
has hardened or if the hairs stayed long
on my shaggy legs, when the sand has so often grated
on my soles and brambles have scratched me while
I walked? Sometimes I bound through the forest, now race
over the main, travel alternately
across land and water. Breasts confined under iron
mail and often hit by spears
or javelins couldn't grow soft to the touch as with you,
who are covered by a mantle or delicate robe.
Neither spindle nor baskets of wool have given tasks
for my hands, only weapons dripping with slaughter.'

Signe did not hesitate to connive in the pretence and back up his assertions; she replied that it was natural for hands which were used to managing wounds more often than wool, fights rather than fleeces, to display a corresponding coarseness. You would not expect them to be limp with the yielding softness of a girl's nor smooth to others' fingers. They had been hardened partly by the toils of war, partly by seafaring habits. It wasn't the custom of one of Haki's warrior slaves to devote herself to women's chores but to hurl spears and lances with a blood-stained right arm. There was no cause to marvel if her soles had stiffened throught pacing out long distances; they had been bruised by the rough shingle every time she ran along the beaches and had become tough with calluses, not tender to feel like theirs. Their feet had never gone far, but had been perpetually confined within the thresholds of the court.

When Hagbarth on the pretext that he was to have the choicest place of rest had taken Signe as his bedfellow, amid their words of shared delights he softly began to address her:

'Say your father caught
and condemned me to a melancholy
fate, will you ever forget
Your promises and seek
a husband after my death?
If that misfortune occurs,
I have no hope of forgiveness,
for your father will spare no pity
in the revenge of his sons.
I killed your brothers after
stripping them of their sea-power,
and now, unknown to your father,
as if I had never done anything
to thwart his wishes, I hold you
here, sharing my bed.
Tell me, my only love,
what kind of desire you will cherish,
without my accustomed embraces.'

Signe answered:

'Believe me, my darling, I want to die together
with you, if Fate presents your requital
first, nor do I wish to prolong my length

of days when mournful Death has driven
you to the tomb. If you should close your eyes
for ever, victim to the savage wills
of executioners, or what ever doom stifles
your breath whether illness, the sword, on water
or soil, I relinquish all wanton and shameful passions,
to vow myself to a similar end,
so that those whom the bed's contract bound together
may be linked by the same fatal suffering.
Even should I feel death's pains, I shall not desert
the man I reckoned worth my love,
who plucked from my mouth its earliest kisses and took
the first-fruits of my tender virginity.
If a woman's voice carries credence, I belive
no promise was ever more certain to last.'

Her words proved such a tonic to Hagbarth's mind that he calculated the pleasure he derived from her vow greater than the peril which lay in his departure.

However, he was betrayed by the young serving-women and set upon by Sigar's henchmen, though he fought long and stubbornly to defend himself and cut many of them to pieces in the doorway. At last he was taken and led to the assembly where he found that the people were divided in their judgments. A number declared he should be punished for such a serious outrage; but Bilvis, brother of Bolvis, together with other advocates of a milder sentence, counselled that instead of treating him ruthlessly they should put his active vigour to good service. Then Bolvis, stepping forward, stressed that it was injurious advice which urged the king to pardon when retribution was imperative, and let misplaced pity soothe down an honest outburst of rage. How could Sigar be moved to spare or commiserate with someone who had robbed him of the twin consolation of his sons and splattered him with the insult of a debauched daughter? This sentiment was approved by the majority of the assembly, Hagbarth condemned and a gibbet erected to receive him. So it transpired that, whereas previously hardly anybody had put forward a harsh vote, a savage sentence was now the general wish.

Soon afterwards the queen proffered a cup, telling him to slake his thirst, and then hurled taunts and threats at him.

'Now arrogant Hagbarth,
judged fit to die by the whole

assembly, put this horn
goblet to your mouth
and taste its thirst-dispelling
liquor. Repress your fears,
now that you are facing
the last hour of life,
and sip this mortal cup
with bold lips, so that
its draught may steer you to
the underworld regions,
where you shall come to the prison
palace of stern Death,
your body given to the gallows,
but your soul consigned below!'

Then the young man, grasping the goblet he had been offered, is said to have given this reply:

'I shall take hold of this final cup,
my last drink, with the very hand
which did away with your twin sons.
I shall not visit the unearthly country
and its fierce ghosts, unavenged. It was
my effort that accomplished their defeat
and locked them in infernal caverns. This right
arm dripped with your family blood,
deprived your offspring of their boyhood years;
those whom your womb had brought forth to the light
were not spared by my funereal sword.
Notorious woman, distracted in mind,
ill-starred mother, bereaved of your children,
time will never restore them to you,
no day nor age will ever give back
the lads my stark death-dealing removed.'

Recompensing her threats of extinction with taunts about her slain sons, he flung back the cup at the queen and drenched her face in a spray of wine.

Meanwhile Signe asked her weeping maids whether they could endure to become the associates of her venture. They replied that they would perform any wish that was in their lady's mind, and subsequently kept their word.

With tears streaming she wanted to follow in death the only partner she had ever had to her bed and ordered that, as soon as the signal had been given from the watch tower, they should fire the bed-chamber with torches, make nooses of their gowns, tie these round their throats and, by kicking away the footstools, strangle themselves. When they concurred, she poured them wine to diminish their fear of death.

Next Hagbarth was brought to be hanged on the hill which afterwards took his name. In order to test his mistress's loyalty, he asked the hangmen to hoist up his mantle, alleging that it would give him satisfaction could he gaze on some image which afforded a preview of his coming death. When they carried out his request, the watchman on the tower thought they were finishing off Hagbarth and signified what he had seen to the girls who were enclosed within the palace. Shortly after, they set the building alight, thrust away the wooden supports under their feet and let the halters twist tight around their necks. Hagbart, seeing the palace swathed in fire and the familiar bedroom blazing, declared that his joy in perceiving his sweetheart's faithfulness was greater than the misery of his own approaching end. He also called upon the assistants to put him to death and testified how little importance he attached to his fate by singing this song:

'Quick, fellows, seize me, swing me into the air!
It is sweet, my bride, to die after your
departure. There are the halls rosy with crackling
fire; now your love reveals its long
agreement, your firm vows are fulfilled, and you
shall be my consort in death as in life.
A single end for us both, one union after;
our first love cannot perish at random.
Happy am I to be blest with such a companion,
and not go miserably to the nether gods
alone. Come, let this knot squeeze the middle of my throat!
This final pain can bring me nothing
but pleasure, for my beloved's restoration is certain,
and death will soon bring its own delight.
Each world has its joy, both will proclaim a mutual
rest for our spirits, faith in love.
See, I willingly accept the decisive moment you offer,
since not even among the shades
does love let a partner disappear from its embrace.'

After these words the hangmen did their work and the noose dispatched him.

Should anyone incline to believe that the traces of antiquity have vanished entirely, proof exists locally that this story is true. The deceased Hagbarth left his name to a village situated not far from Sigar's town; there a mound rising slightly above the plain, like a bulge in the earth, indicates old foundations by its measurements. Someone reported to Archbishop Absalon that he had seen a beam which a peasant had discovered in that spot when his ploughshare struck it as he was turning up the soil.

Saxo Grammaticus, Love and Law. The Tale of Hagbard and Signe

NIELS HENRIK HOLMQVIST-LARSEN

The object of this contribution to the theme of the seminar is one of the most beloved tales of Danish medieval literature: the tale of Hagbard and Signe by the learned Saxo Grammaticus - the clerk of Archbishop Absalon - in his Gesta Danorum, the Latin History of Denmark written in the decades around the year 1200.

Before reading any further, please enjoy the text as it is quoted in this anthology in Peter Fisher's English translation.[1]

A tale about tragic love

The tale is the most famous tragic love-story of medieval Denmark. It is a tale comparable to the story of *Romeo and Juliet*: two young people are passionately in love, but their happiness is illicit and impossible because of a family feud. In Saxo's description it is a virtual Viking vendetta.

I shall not enter into a discussion of the various ideas and meanings of the terms Love or Law; but I hope to offer some comments on the tale which will elucidate the medieval construction of the concept of Marriage as a love-match. A construction from which we incurably suffer.

The background

The tale has been known for a long time in Denmark as well as in the other Nordic countries. We know from small hints in scaldic poems that it has been told perhaps since the ninth century, but Saxo's text is the oldest version preserved. After Saxo, the motif was used in the so-called popular ballads known from the sixteenth century onwards - and in one version with a very outspoken morale: 'It is a good thing, that when a young man wants to woo, he talks to the father and to the mother of his beloved otherwise it can turn out very sadly'. The popularity of the tale is also indicated by the amount of learned or 'learned' explanations of place-names connected with the tale in both Denmark, Norway and Sweden. It was also used in Denmark as a patriotic and moral fable during the century of Enlightenment. Eventually it became a subject for national romanticist paintings, and even a theme for a high-strung 'erotic tragedy' in 1815 by the 'Nordic King of Poets' Adam Oehlenschläger.[2] More recently, the tale was the subject for a movie - *The Red Cloak* by Gabriel Axel in 1967 - which at the time was rather famous for its nude scenes.

The tale has thus been part of popular and learned beliefs - used in historical writings, in Enlightenment morality, in the birth of Danish national feeling, in the romanticist movement - and it played a (very minor) role in the 'sexual revolution'. It is certainly part of the Danish cultural heritage. But why this popularity?

The actors of the tale

Everybody has probably had the experience not being able to get the one he or she is in love with. The Hagbard and Signe-story is about real people and not an exotic *fairy tale*. The motif of the story lies in the personalities of the principal characters and in their conflict with social demands. The forces working in the story are recognizable human phenomena: desire, jealousy, slander, bribery, revenge - and love and law.

Hagbard

Hagbard is rather dull. A real Saxo-hero of royal blood: strong, brave, prudent and in accordance with Saxo's aristocratic and clerically inspired moral universe. In a condensed version this universe could be characterized as the ethos of the King's *housecarls* in a Christian setting - and it could be expressed in the following well-known medieval terms:

The Cardinal Virtues:
- *Fortitudo* - bravery
- *Temperantia* - temperance
- *Iustitia* - justice

- *Prudentia* - prudence

and the Christian Virtues:
- *Fides* - faith
- *Spes* - hope
- *Caritas* - charity

Hagbard is above all courageous, a great warrior and a man of honour. He follows the codes that bid him revenge his brothers; unfortunately, he is also in love with Signe, who has 'promised to be his mistress secretly'. After killing her brothers in an appropriately noble fight he wants to see this promise fulfilled. Saxo describes Hagbard's interest in Signe with the words: *Adeo Libido periculum contemnit* - 'This is the extent to which desire makes light of danger'. Libido is the keyword. Initially Hagbard is only sexually interested in Signe - and as Saxo was no Victorian it is perfectly in order for a (secular) man to be sexually infatuated with a woman.

Hagbard's personality is probably best described through the picture of his opponent: the highranking, handsome, yellow-bellied, treacherous, German specimen of a court vermin, Hildegisl, who is described as so hopelessly unmanly that he gets wounded in the buttocks when escaping from the fight, a wound of infamy. In Icelandic laws this *klamhögg* - cut of shame - is comparable only to castration, judging by the size of the fines and the inherent disgrace. Hildegisl is a nidding, an immoral non-male; if one has received a wound like this - was the belief - one can be used sexually by other men ('phallic agression').[3] Naturally, Hagbard is the absolute opposite: The ideal male.

Signe

Signe, on the other hand, is quite different from the usual Saxo-women. They are more or less like the Queen of Hearts: beautiful, but one-dimensional and stereotyped persons to whom something may happen, but who do not act themselves. Signe acts: she despises the socially acceptable but morally unworthy marriage with the infamous Hildegisl. Hagbard has the moral male qualities that awakens her love. His *virtus* pulls the trigger; Signe is not a person that Hagbard can entice or seduce: she chooses him herself, and her love is so passionate and yet carefully considered that it defies all obstacles.

In spite of her obstinacy in relation to the demands of her family, Signe demonstrates *temperantia*: in her self-knowledge she realizes that society (as expressed by Saxo) seldom trusts the word of a woman.

She also shows *prudentia*: she helps Hagbard, disguised as a shield-maiden, carrying through the deception of the female servants. Moreover, she shows *fortitudo*: like an antique heroine she chooses suicide when her lover dies. Even so, although she shows several of the Cardinal Virtues, her main characteristic is one of the *Christian* Virtues: *fides* - faith.

Signe is not like Saxo's more spectacular active women: the *shield-maidens*; she is not a creature dangerous to men. Signe faithfully accepts her role as an ordinary woman. Her moral greatness is that she is able to carry the burden of this role under her special circumstances - even to the bitter end. It is obviously this faith that makes Hagbard love her, not just desiring her. Hagbard tests her - 'he asked the hangmen to hoist up his mantle...' - and she acts so that he in his magnificent death poem can conclude that they were *par in amore fides* - they had mutual faith in Love. For Signe, moral virtue is the reason for loving Hagbard - and for Hagbard it is the knowledge of Signe's faithfulness that makes him love her. To Saxo, I guess, this is the ideal content of the roles of the two sexes when in love. The irony of the story - and the tragedy - is that their high moral standards cause their death. His honour and bravery forces him to revenge his brothers and her loyalty forces her to keep her promise and love none but him.[4]

Love

Hagbard and Signe go to bed together; they have sexual intercourse. Then follows one of the climaxes of the story: the *voluptatis colloqvia* - "a conversation of love and lust"; *voluptas* has exactly this carnal connotation. During the conversation both of them stress that their relationship is *marriage* - and consequently not adultery. They talk about their *foedus tori* - 'covenant of the conjugal bed' - *coniugii fides* - 'the loyalty of marriage' and Hagbard calls Signe *nupta* - 'my wife'. They express their wish to die together because the revenge of Signe's father king Sigar will surely come. Signe closes the conversation: 'Even should I feel death's pains, I shall not desert the man I reckoned worth my love, who plucked the first-fruits of my tender virginity. If a woman's voice carries credence, I believe no promise was ever more certain to last'.

Law

Hagbard and Signe actually seem to accept the law of the family; it is inevitable that they must die because of their love. Their child - if they had one - could bring social chaos. The child could be tempted to revenge either his mother's brothers or his father and his brothers. The result of such ill-fated relations is actually exposed in some of the Icelandic Family Sagas.[5]

Eventually, her maids betray them and Hagbard kills many of king Sigar's *house-carls* before he is captured. Saxo says that when Hagbard was first brought to court, his fate was undecided. However the evil Bölvis, Hildegisl's bribed creature, turns the tables. His rhetoric fixes on Hagbard's killing of the king's sons, and on the insult to Sigar through the 'debauched and seduced daughter': 'A savage sentence was now the general wish'.

After the death of Hagbard and Signe, the vendetta goes on: Hagbard's older brother takes revenge. And in the end, the only survivor of royal Danish blood is king Sigar's infant, female grandchild; but the restitution of the royal line is another story.

Saxo and his Tale

Saxo's own attitude towards the tale is twofold: he has difficulty in accepting the structure of the tale and the unavoidable blood-feud and consequent death of Hagbard and Signe. He is so fascinated by his ideal couple that he stresses the great influence of the evil persons of Hildegisl and Bölvis who in his version of the story first provoke the fighting and then the 'savage sentence'. *They* are the guilty ones. But - regrettably - Hagbard and Signe are the actors who must die.

In this story Saxo is about to accept something which he would not normally accept: that love is more important than social demands. In the *Gesta Danorum* there are about one hundred stories concerning marriages. Most of them are 'normal'. The girls are given away in marriage by their fathers, given as rewards, prizes etc. and nobody asks them what they feel. Fourteen of the one hundred decide for themselves. Of these, three are monstrous women in opposition to the order of the world: one is actually a giantess. Only three of the remaining eleven are described fully and as *great* women - loyal to their men in life as in death: Signe belongs to an absolute minority.

Usually Saxo does not believe in women. He writes in the Hamlet story:

'Every female vow is stolen away by changes of fortune or evaporates with shifting seasons, a woman's reliability stands on slippery soles and is weakened by chance accidents. Her faith is glibly pledged but executed slowly; hampered by the various allurements of pleasure. Always eager to seek out new interests and forget the old, it leaps away, breathlessly, towards its desire'.[6]

It was probably statements like this that made the Danish historian A.D. Jørgensen write in 1871 that Saxo - because of his 'unmarried status' - lacked 'the bright view of the finest peculiarities of female nature'.[7] Actually Saxo also states that in the old days women chose their own husbands. He tells about the golden days of king Frode Fredegod - 'the Peacemaker' - the king even promulgated a law - Saxo applauds it as *bonae artes* - decreeing that women had individual rights in deciding their marriages. This story is, however, immediately followed by other stories, in which these rights are not used or thought of at all.[8]

Canon law and marriage

Is there more to the extraordinary *love* of Signe or to Frode's law of marriage and Saxo's various proclamations of the rights of women?

I believe that the French historian Georges Duby has made an important point. In some of his works[9] he has advocated the existence of two opposing views of marriage in the Middle Ages: the secular/aristocratic and the clerical/canonical. The interests of the old aristocratic society were of course centred around legitimate children and the inheritance of landed property, while the clerical view had to do with the status of marriage as a sacrament: force must not be involved before God.

Therefore, the fight between these two opposite 'world views' was primarily about *divorce* - a necessity in dynastic policy involving alliances between families. In contrast, the Church's individualizing ideology furthermore allowed *matrimonium clandestinum*, 'secret marriage' when the parties had given their *consensus* and showed *maritalis affectio* - 'marital affection'. As the famous canonist Gratian put it in 1140: *nuptias non concubitus, sed consensus facit* - 'it is consensus, not sleeping together that creates a marriage'.

Secret marriage was eventually forbidden by the Fourth Lateran Council in 1215, as part of a compromise, but it did not as a consequence become invalid. The parties would only be made to pay a fine to the Church.[10]

This laxity in a matter of great economic interest to the heads of families provoked of course shrewd restrictions and regulations. It was far too easy for young people - and others in family custody - to enter into legally and economically binding relationships. The responsible elders had to take their measures when it became clear how lenient the Church was towards the individual choice of spouses.

Georges Duby writes:

> *'The entire history of marriage in Western Christendom amounts to a gradual process of acculturation, in which the ecclesiastical model slowly gained the upper hand, not over disorder - as is too often claimed by those who blindly espouse the point of view of Churchmen whose testimony is almost all that has come down to us - but over a different order, one that was solidly entrenched and not easily dislodged'.*[11]

Marriage in medieval Danish law

This other order is the order found in Old Danish Society - the society of Saxo. Marriage was, of course, a private family matter, but *Canon Law* - the law of the Church - became more and more influential. This called for compromises with the provincial laws, such as the *Scanian Law* from around 1200. These casuistic, secular and private collections of legal directions had no rules at all about Marriage, whereas *Canon Law* obviously, among other social bonds, also was supposed to regulate Marriage. But the youngest of the Danish provincial laws, *The Jutish Law* of 1241 - promulgated some 20 years after Saxo finished his chronicle - surprisingly contains new regulations on 'How to marry': it must be with the consent of the woman (the *consensus*) and her male relatives. The law states in a preceding chapter that: 'A brother cannot keep his sister unmarried with him as long as he wants, but if a brother wants to keep his sister with him or any other kinsman a woman, for whom he is guardian, because of her money, when she is more than eighteen winters and kinsmen testify that they could provide her a suitable marriage, then her closest kinsmen shall complain to the King, and the King can then with their advice marry her away ....'. In other words: guardians cannot keep their wards from marrying just to keep their money or property at their own disposal, but the consent and good will of the male members of the family is still crucial when it comes to marriage.[12]

The chapters on marriage of *The Jutish Law* show not just influence of principles of *Canon Law*. Another principle - probably based on tradition - is also discernible in the law-book. *Marriage by Prescription* is made a legal institute in *The Jutish Law*. This prescription is a provisional and uncanonical relationship that after a period of three years - during which 'divorce' is possible - becomes a legally valid marriage. In principle - with this singular exception - the law accepts the canonical point of view that divorce is not possible.[13]

The concessions of the law to the views of the Church on marriage, however, actually turns out to be purely superficial: there are no sanctions if women are forced into marriage or if they are kept unmarried by their guardians. In reality, *The Jutish Law* pays lipservice to *Canon Law*. Confronted with the danger of ecclesiastical eagerness in propagating individual solutions, the patriarchal pillars of society probably felt themselves forced to use the secular laws to uphold at least some of the old and - to them - necessary positions.

The Jutish Law was promulgated by king Valdemar, and several of the bishops of Denmark were witnesses. But bishops were pragmatists - and they were aristocrats themselves. They knew the difficulties of everyday life and the value of working compromises.

Saxo, love and marriage

Saxo is part of the same compromise or acculturation: on the surface - as a churchman - he can praise *consensus* as a kind of 'feminine liberty', but in reality it is only a super-woman like Signe that makes him give up his patriarchal ideas and reconsider 'female freedom'. I believe that Saxo in the wording of his text means to give his contemporary, learned readers - Saxo's readers were of course all learned - a feeling that these wonderful young people were *not* adulterous, and although they lived in the heathen past, they had acted in a way that in his own day would be acceptable to the Holy Church - that is, acceptable before the canonical steps taken against clandestine marriage in 1215. We even have a *terminus technicus* from *Canon Law* for Hagbard's and Signe's kind of marriage: *Sponsalia per verba de presenti* - 'an engagement and agreement on immediate marriage' - and where the marriage becomes valid when *coitus* has taken place. Saxo seems to stress that Hagbard and Signe did not live in the flesh alone: they really had a marital affection for one another in his version of the tale.

This suggestion has recently been strenghtened in a brilliant analysis by the philologist and Saxo-specialist, Karsten Friis Jensen, who in Saxo's story of Hagbard and Signe has found so many hidden verbal and metrical quotations from 'The Marriage between Mercury and Philology' by Martianus Capella (5th century A.D.) that he can say that the text basically 'signals marriage'.[14] The story of Hagbard and Signe shows Saxo's reluctant acceptance of individual choice as a basis for marriage and an acceptance of mutual love as part of marriage as a legal institution.

In this way Saxo's story is also a step in the process of the gradual acculturation in Western Europe where *Love* - when it comes to marriage - becomes ideologically integrated in the understanding of *Law* so that a marriage not founded on love gets at least a tinge of the improper and illegal.

Notes:

1 The story from Saxo's Book VII is told on pp. 212-18 of the translation: H.E.Davidson and P. Fisher, *The History of the Danes*. Book I-X, Vol.I (English text), Vol. II (Comments), Bury St.Edmunds 1980. The standard edition of the Latin text is *Saxonis Gesta Danorum*, T.I (Text), (eds.) J.Olrik & H.Ræder, Cph. 1931, T.II (*Index verborum*) (ed.) Franz Blatt, Cph. 1957. The present paper is based on my book, *Møer, skjoldmøer og krigere. En studie i og omkring 7. Bog af Saxo's Gesta Danorum*, (Studier fra Sprog- og Oldtidsforskning, 304) Cph. 1983, especially pp. 72-103.

2 F.Jonsson (ed.), *Den norsk-islandske Skjaldedigtning*, Vol. B.I, Cph. 1912 (repr. 1967), p. 9, 239 and 287. S. Grundtvig (ed.), *Danmarks gamle Folkeviser*, Vol. 1, Cph. 1853 (repr. 1966), no. 20, p. 258-317. Quotation from p. 304. [P.F.Suhm], 'Signe og Habor eller Kierlighed stærkere end Døden', in *Forsøg i de skiønne og nyttige Videnskaber. Samlede ved et patriotisk Selskab.* 12. Stykke, Cph. 1777. p. 93-215. A.Oehlenschläger, Hagbarth og Signe, Cph. 1815. K.Monrad, *Mellem guder og helte. Historiemaleriet i Rom, Paris og København* 1770-1820, Cph. 1990.

3 P.Meulengracht Sørensen, *The Unmanly Man: Concepts of Sexual Defamation in early Northern Society*, Odense 1983.

4 During the discussion after the lecture it was commented that another theme of the story was *disguises* and *fraud* and that both Hagbard and Signe only act when they are convinced that the other is dead. Signe awaits the sign of the cloak and Hagbard the firing of Signe's house: it seems a kind of love's 'mutual distrust' and a wish to be 'last player' - wrapped up in fatal irony, but it is only a secondary motif.

5 T.Bredsdorff, *Kaos og Kærlighed. En studie i islændingesagaernes livsbillede*, Cph. 1971. See also: K. Hastrup, 'Kinship in Medieval Iceland', Folk, Vol. 23, Cph. 1981.

6 Saxo, Book IV, Fisher's translation p. 101.
7 A.D.Jørgensen, 'Saxe, Absalons klerk', in idem, *Bidrag til Nordens Historie i Middelalderen*, Cph. 1871.
8 The 'Laws of Frode': Saxo, Book V, Fisher's translation, p. 143.
9 George Duby, *Medieval Marriage. Two Models from Twelfth Century France*, Baltimore and London 1978, and *The Knight, the Lady and the Priest. The Making of Modern Marriage in Medieval France*, Penguin ed. 1983.
10 See J.T.Noonan, 'Power to choose', *Viator, 4, 1973*, and idem, 'Marital Affection in the Canonists', *Collectanea Stephan Kuttner II, Studia Gratiana*, T.12, Bologna 1967.
11 Duby, Two Models, p. 17.
12 The Jutish Law, Part I, Book I, Chapters 8 (brothers and sisters) and 33 (how to marry). E. Kroman & S. Juul (translators), *Skaanske Lov og Jyske Lov*. 4. impression, Cph. 1968.
13 The Jutish Law, Part I, Book I, Chapters 27 *(marriage by prescription)* and 24 *(divorce not possible)*.
14 K.Friis-Jensen, 'Hagbarth and Signe, Saxo's star-crossed lovers', in A.Cipolla (ed.), *L'immaginario nelle Letterature Germaniche del Medioevo*, Milano 1995.

Legal Cultures, Affection and Community

DITLEV TAMM

In a recent book 'Poetic Justice' (1995) Martha Nussbaum has a quite interesting reading of Dickens' novel 'Hard Times'.[1] A chief character of the novel is Mr. Gradgrind who in Nussbaum's reading becomes a symbol of lack of imagination: 'In this life, we want nothing but Facts, sir, nothing but Facts', is one of the typical Gradgrind phrases. Lawyers very often, and Nussbaum emphazises that especially those of the American Law and Economics School, can appear as Gradgrinds. Law however is not just facts and lawyers not necessarily Gradgrinds. That is what I will try to show from a more traditional legal historian's point of view. But it shall be admitted that law has and probably must have quite a lot of Gradgrind facts in it.

Two quotations can illustrate my point:
'If you kill my slave, I think that personal feelings should not be taken into account...' Thus the Roman jurist Paul wrote sometime in the beginning of the 3rd century A.D.[2]

'How can one evaluate sentiments and passions. It is impossible', said the 19th century Belgian lawyer François Laurent.[3]

Rome was a slave society and quite a bit of Roman law is about slaves. Roman lawyers could not be blamed for sentimentality. There is not much about feelings in Roman law. Basically law and feelings were considered distinct areas. In this respect Roman law is modern. When today's lawyer tends to exclude that emotions play an important role in law he is sticking to a tradition that goes back to Roman law. Francois Laurent who treated the French civil Code is just another link in this chain.

The tradition however has not been unbroken. The influence of Christianity on the law in the late Antique made mutual love and fraternity part of the lawyers' universe. The so called golden rule - that you shall love your neighbour as yourself and do to others what you want them to do to you - was a starting point for deliberations as to right and wrong in the law. All law lives from love, Luther said referring himself to Augustin. Luther blamed the lawyers for their lack of love: 'Juristen böse Christen', he said, lawyers are bad Christians. The aim, life and force of all law is peace, love and unity, he stated in 1517.[4]

The quotation I made above from Roman law was about the special affections that someone could have towards a slave and therefore could be expected to buy that slave at a higher price than his or her market value. Such affections could not be taken into account by the assessment of the slave. Only economic interests. That is one of the legacies of the Late Antiquity to modern law. Lawyers often tend to consider it a distinction of the good lawyer that he can keep sense and sensibility separated.

Affections or latin 'affectus' was also the word used by the Romans when they talked of marriage. Not too much law was a characteristic of Roman marital law. The most common Roman marriage was the so called 'free marriage'. It was easy to enter and easy to dissolve. It only subsisted as long as the 'affectus maritalis', i.e. a feeling or reciproque will to maintain the connection was there. It need not be love. When the affectus disappeared then marriage went too. Christianity changed the traditional Roman pattern. Canon law gave rules for entering marriage and put serious obstacles to getting out of it again. Canon law as it developed in the Middle Ages is a legal system that clearly reflects relations between love and law.

Marriage without love, however, seems to have prevailed. The family took care of that. The Church had another point of view. Marriage was a relation between man and woman who both had to consent: 'Nuptias ... consensus facit'.[5] It is consent that establishes marriage. The old feudal way of arranging marriages met with the new idea propagated by the Church. The influence of the Church in the Middle Ages has been characterized as the papal revolution. Feelings had to be taken into consideration - but not unconditionally.

In one of the medieval Danish written laws, the Law of Jutland from 1241 we see how two different ways of thinking met. Marriage of a woman was arranged by the next male akin. But it is expressly stated that he must act in accordance with her consent - as demanded by the Church. No force to enter this sacrament. Probably the Law of Jutland was written down by clerics. But the family maintained a remedy to force the dissident woman. If she married against the will of the family she lost her property. Freedom to let oneself govern by feelings had a price - then as today.

The time around 1200 is sometimes known as the 'century of love' full of troubadours and their 'cours d'amour',[6] the century of 'il dolce stil nuovo' and a new poetry of love. That same period is among lawyers known as the 'juridical century'. In the decades preceding and following 1200 European law had a new fundament. On a European level we can see the renaissance of Roman law and the pope as legislator. On the national level we find new written laws as the just mentioned Law of Jutland.

Love played a central role in Canon law that developed in those years into a universal legal system. Christianity is a religion of love. Mercy and clemency, the love of God are central concepts - gratia, clementia and caritas in Latin. We still know some of those concepts from our legal vocabulary as pardon, mitigation of punishment or remission of debt.

Love according to the canonists, those lawyers that had Canon law as their field, was not a necessary condition for marriage but a consequence of marriage. The chief scope of marriage was procreation. Attraction to the canonists normally was physical not love. Marriage however was not just the junction of two bodies. It was also the junction of the souls in a permanent friendship 'firma amicitia', to want and not want the same things 'idem velle et nolle'[7] - which, as those experienced in human relations will know, is often easier to say than to practice. Marriage was not just a contract as in Roman law. The Canonist did not seem insensitive to influence from comtemporary poetry and theology. Marriage was developing into an emotional relation.

Love however should not be exaggerated according to some of the leading Church fathers. Especially Saint Jerome from the time around 400 had a great authority. He was against sexual life and marriage. It was not good, he once wrote, if a man loved his wife too much. He could then tend to exaggerate physical intercourse and that was lascivious and thus a deformity. To Jerome love and sexuality seemed identical. There is no greater wrong than to have sexual intercourse with your wife as if she were another woman. Not too often and not too much were his rules. Saint Jerome did quite a job to promote Western European sense of guilt in connection with sex. Not to speak of just those outer signs that could lead to extramarital sex. No bathing together, no touching and definitely no kissing.

In China a few years ago ago I wondered about the meaning of a sign in the public parks showing two lips barred by a red line until I realised that it meant: No kissing. We can see how different cultures feel the importance of controlling peoples' feelings. Love and Justice were intimately related in the medieval idea of law. Law was seen as an acting part of love. Selfishness was a starting point - you must love yourself in order to be able to love others and to be able to pursue the supreme good. You could even make a system of love according to its objects, yourself, man, wife, children, your neighbour, your country or justice. Today we could continue by adding new objects as love of nature, the European Union a.s.o. Still in the 17th century Swedish lawyers could write of 'the importance of love toward yourself'.[8] Reading of moral treatises, theological works with speculation of the essence of love and the theological and the secular virtues counting justice as an important example was part of a good lawyer's education at that time when a high degree of specialization was not seen as an absolute advantage. Personal 'habitus' was important for those who as lawyers should administer an order that ultimately based itself on divine love.

Marriage and the law of marriage easily play a dominant role in a discussion of law and emotions. In criminal law however we know the concept of 'crime passionel' - the emotive crime. Our own criminal law is not insensitive to emotions. If a crime is committed under the impression of strong emotions it can according to the Danish Penal Code be taken into consideration.

When lawyers today talk of feelings they often think of a certain sense of justice that has to be considered if rules are to be followed. 'The first requirement of a sound body of law is that it should correspond with actual feelings and demands of the community, whether right or wrong', the famous American lawyer Oliver Wendell Holmes said.[9]

Law and emotions are in fact more closely linked than you might think when you listen to the Roman jurist Paul quoted in the beginning of this essay. The centuries of love and law coincided. The law does take emotions into consideration.

Literature is often a good guideline to an understanding of some of the emotions that law has to regulate. Law and Literature is a movement that opposes itself to the more barren Law and Economics' view of life.

In the famous scene of Shakespeare's 'The Merchant of Venice' (IV, 1) in which Portia appears disguised as a lawyer to defend Antonio against the claim of 'a pound of flesh' - the strict and harsh interpretation of his contract - she says appealing to Shylock's feelings:

> *'The quality of mercy is not strain'd,*
> *It droppeth as the gentle rain from heaven...' It bless both him that gives and him that receives. It is*
> *'an attribute to God himself,*
> *and earthly power doth then show likest God's,*
> *When mercy seasons Justice'.*

The Jew does not show mercy and - paradoxically - no mercy is bestowed on him. Emotions have their course, as so often in real life.

Lawyers, too, are human beings and governed by their emotions, 'right or wrong', as Holmes said. It was certainly easier to admit to emotions at a time when law was considered a part of God's order of love. I see a seminar like this as a search for a new fundament for letting feelings find their place in law once again. Time will show whether we shall have another century of both love and law.

You cannot live from Justice alone, Aristotle wrote. And the Church father St. Augustin said: When love starts, there is justice, love advanced is justice advanced, great love is great justice, perfect love is perfect justice - '*charitas inchoata iustitia est; charitas magna, magna iustitia; charitas perfecta, perfecta iustitia est*'.[10]

Notes:

1 Martha Nussbaum: *Poetic Justice*, Boston 1995 p. 1 s.
2 Justinians Digest 9,2,33 pr.
3 François Laurent: *Principes du droit français* XV, 3rd ed. 1878, p. 560.
4 'Finis, vita, virtus omnium legum est pax, charitas, concordia', Cp. Johannes Heckel: *Lex Charitatis* 2 ed. 1973, p. 64.
5 See i.a. Justinians Digest 50,17,30.
6 Peter Goodrich: *Law in the Courts of Love*, London 1996, p. 29 s.
7 See to this and the following James A. Brundage: *Law, Sex and Christian Society in Medieval Europe*, UCP 1987, p. 273 and passim.
8 David Nehrmann quoted by Bo H. Lindberg: *Praemia et Poenae* (Stenc.), Uppsala 1992, p. 143.
9 Oliver Wendell Holmes: *The Common Law*, N.Y. 1881, p. 41.
10 Augustin: *De natura et gratia* LXX, quoted by Luis Legal y Lacambra: *El derecho y el amor, Barcelona* 1976, p. 165.

Traditional Latvian Culture: Pragmatism and Love

DAGMARA BEITNERS

Upon first glance one might question, is it possible to attribute the relationship between reason and love as something uniquely characteristic of a certain culture. Love is recognized as a universal expression of effect, and it has become an aspect of European cultural identity. Love has created a shared means of communication, even though the realm of emotion does not belong to any one specific culture or language. At the same time, established cultural stereotypes have influenced the means of expressing love.

First of all the relationship between love and language, the text. In European culture, love as a traditional expression of emotion has been cultivated through the written word; it is the text which influences the spiritual vitality of society. The text has enabled love to become a universal spiritual value, without which it is impossible to imagine contemporary human society.

The intent of this presentation is to address the traditional from a prechristian intuitive stance. Therefore, it is of importance to separate out the Christian perspective, which is expressed in the well known text from Paul's first letter to the Corinthians: 'faith, hope and love, but the greatest of these is love' (13;13), a love which is described as gentle, kind and humble... Of course, this traditional Christian approach has left a significant imprint upon the interpretation of love's meaning within culture.

In his essays on the history of love the Russian poet Jevgenejs Bogats perceived love as civilization's accumulated spiritual heritage, which can be thought of as a segment of the intellectual noosphere. He translates love as a movement created by the soul, culminating at the planetary stratum. This is the romantic and sentimental love which one must seek ideally to fulfil.

One is also reminded of de La Rochefoucauld, who said that "with love it is like seeing ghosts - everyone speaks about it, but only a few have experienced it'. In contemporary culture love is something which everyone is awaiting, which everyone wants to experience. But has this always been so? And has the expression of love's norm always been the same in European culture?

The Baltic countries, including Latvia, are perceived still today by many Westerners as a part of Russia and as all that which was for many decades behind the 'iron curtain'- distant, strange and of little consequence. But these countries historically, culturally and mentally substantiate distinct ethic and linguistic stratum. Even today they have retained many characteristics of their traditional agrarian society, having been for many decades politically separated from contemporary European life. The Baltic cultures contribute a segment to the group of small ethnic unities - and one historian has said that these small ethnic unities are very meaningful to European culture as a whole, and if they did not exist, someone would have to invent them.

Latvia as a coherent ethic unity was formed in the 17th century, as the historical differences between the ancient Latvian tribes - kursi, zemgali, seli and latgali- were becoming negligible. Already since the 13th century the Latvian territory had been successively colonized by the Germans, Swedes, Poles and Russians. The Christianization of the Latvian tribes, consequently, involved the influence of all three churches - the Orthodox, Catholic and Protestant. And although the Latvian ethnos and culture was influenced by the syncretism of both secular and Christian forces, the dominant role was held by the traditional, pagan culture.

A peculiarity of Latvia is that although Christianization had been attempted since the 13th century, it became only during the second part of the 19th century. It is recognized, that at the beginning of the 20th century the Latvian perspective on life and its values was strongly influenced by the 'dainas'.[1] Today they have less direct influence upon Latvian society and literature.

However, in my opinion, indirectly the 'dainas' are continuing to the exert their influence in hidden form upon behavioural stereotypes and value systems.[2]

A marked feature of the Latvian 'dainas', as noted by V.Vike-Freiberga, is the lack of romanticism in the traditional folk wedding songs.[3] In the 'dainas' we do not find romanticized emotion or the sentiment of unfulfilled longing. This seems to be a paradox because the written Latvian literary tradition, which is slightly more than a century and a half old, can be characterized as primarily romantic and lyrical. There was a severing from the traditional culture of the 'dainas', or, more precisely, it was the rapid development of Latvian literature during the second half of the 19th century, facilitated by translations from Western European literary canon.

The lack of romanticism in the 'dainas' does not mean that the Latvian people have been without emotion or have consistently suppressed their emotions in a 'northerly' manner. Folklorists, those who have been concerned with exploring or translating the 'dainas', have always emphasized the sincerity, empathy and tenderness which is present in the 'dainas' which speak of the relationship between parents and their children, or between brothers and sisters. Also in 'dainas' which tell about the surrounding nature we find a tender pastoral poetry, and in descriptions of cosmic relationship there is a similar sincerity or closeness. There are soul-filled emotions regarding one's surroundings, including one's perceptions of God.

I rose early in the morning,
Dear God rose earlier yet.
Why God did you get up,
What did you need so early?

What would you do dear girl,
If I didn't rise early?
I open the doors for you,
I give you all advice.
LD 33668

Then why do the 'dainas' not speak of romantic love, if they already possess such sincerity and tenderness, which is accentuated by the common use of the diminutives. But a close reading of 'dainas' reveals that emotions are also expressed through that which is spoken indirectly: 'I sewed a linen shirt all summer - but it didn't go to the one for whom it was sewn, and I gave it to another while shedding tears'(7394) tells about a young maiden who is not ruler of her destiny, her emotional world or her choice of husband.

V.Vike-Freiberga applies the analysis of McLuhan's 'cool' and 'hot' medium of communication and finds that the 'dainas' belong to the 'cool' information structures, in the depths of which is found encoded a broad specter of emotion - from the tragic to the comic. Such a means of distancing, as will be illustrated, will be characteristic in the other spectre of relationship between love and language as found in the Latvian 'dainas'.

It is most possible that tradition for Latvian marriage was largely based upon practical, pragmatic concerns, which had little to do with personal emotions as we interpret them today. This ignoring of feeling is known in European culture from ancient Greek times, and this model of marriage still today is referred to as a calculated betrothal. In the 'dainas' one hears these pragmatic concerns: 'I am not looking at young body, but am looking at your fields, to see if there is grain to make bread'(LD 25912).

The choice of one's marriage partner was often made by parents, or by brothers or sisters, who had greater opportunity to become familiarized with the future in-law. Not always did this choice coincide with that which was felt through the heart: 'The marches are frozen the lakes are frozen. With a frozen heart I am going to give my hand in marriage'(LD 75458).

During the 700 years that the Latvian people had been subjugated to colonizing forces, this created a cultural self-enclosure whereby certain legal norms which were no longer common in the rest of Europe were preserved. Since marriages often took place without taking into consideration emotion, then there was established the norm that the brother could visit his betrothed sister, and if he found his sister unhappy, then he could return her to the parental home: 'I brought back the float of swans from the muddy swamp; I brought back my sister from the drunken young man'.

As another example, still in the 17th century, the governor of Livland, Uksenchern, imposed a law of capital punishment for the abduction of a bride. Professor H.Biezais notes that 100 years after the Reformation the Latvians still practised such a barbaric means of obtaining a bride.[4]

When in the 18th century the Latvians were increasingly more dependently subjugated to their manor lords, such abusive marriages even further removed the Latvian peasants from that model of emotional life which was proliferated in Western Europe, and which was based upon the priority of love in preference to reason.

It is interesting that the Baltic Germans living in Latvia cultivated the tradition of romantic and sentimental love known in Western Europe. However, the Baltic German manor lords and the Latvian peasants were separated by such a deep social rift that the Latvians did not assimilate the model of emotional life which was flaunted by their oppressors.

Returning to the 'dainas' we can say that we find in them a strong cultural tradition which serves to make less painful the acute harshness of life and suffering, also through the suppression of feeling, not allowing their harsh emotions to become realized. They are more or less distanced, at times ironic, at times laughing. They have strength and vitality.

Folklore research of the 'dainas' has noted that the greater portion has been generated and perpetuated by Latvian women. The 'dainas' carry within them the spiritual dominance of women vertically and horizontally, as is characteristic of agrarian culture. We find that Latvian traditional culture was patriarchal in that the bride went to the home of her husband, and that emotional life in the modern sense was attributed little significance. But this situation has also created also an entire genre of erotic 'dainas' which have been assembled under the heading 'the naughty dainas'.[5]

These 'naughty' or bawdy 'dainas' indicate that Latvians have been interested in addressing the more erotic aspects of love. In the oral tradition these 'dainas' have maintained their place with the others, regardless of the fact that the Christian church fathers desired to influence the Latvian people and to assimilate them to their Christian norms of morality. These 'naughty dainas' constitute an entire tradition, which is referred to by the Germans as 'gesunde Erotik', healthy eroticism, where all is referred to by its actual name, while yet maintaining the traditional quatrain structure. In their poetic imagery they can be compared to the literary direction of D. Boccacio and F. Rablais.

Most interesting is that the erotic or bawdy dainas have also been largely generated by women. The Latvian poet K. Skujenieks has half-jokingly commented that even in creating these 'dainas' the women had the greatest fantasy. The 'dainas' are always difficult to translate, but we can make some approximation: 'My dear spotted cow, we both have a difficult life - you are butchered to death, I am butted while still alive'.

Psychologist S. Sebre has noted that these bawdy 'dainas' are in their sarcastic form of expression emotionally distanced, as if spoken from a separate vantage point. Sebre has implied that there is some relationship in affective tone to the descriptions given by women who have suffered from sexual abuse - that all which is experienced they viewed as if from a point removed. In the 'dainas' the sexual experience is presented with light humour, at times exaggerated.

In the Latvian culture there is not noted any contrast between the sacred and profane. The Christian idea of sin, as evidenced in historical texts, was never accepted or understood by the Latvians. Not only from the 'dainas', but also from the Church records we know that the Latvians practised what was known as 'trial marriage'. Upon the reprimands and threats of the pastor, they responded that they are not doing anything wrong, and that among Latvians this is accepted.

Looking from this perspective, traditional Latvian society seems pragmatic in respect to love and romantic feeling, but more sensitive regarding the erotic aspects. But one cannot say the same of contemporary Latvian culture. Many of the moral norms have been likened to Western cultural norms. However, there is some continuity which has been revealed in a questionnaire completed in the early 90s by Latvian women of various ages. They responded in answer to the questions: What do you consider as the most important in relationships between men and women? The answers were compiled as follows: respect 35%; understanding 21%; faithfulness 13%; love 12,4%; friendship 4%; sexual harmony 2,6%, spiritual harmony 2,4%.[6]

As we can see, love is ranked as fourth in importance - Latvian women even today value more highly than romantic feeling those pragmatic aspects which are essential to living together and creating a unified family life. This is very important for a small ethnic group, which at various times in its history has been threatened by demographic extinction.

Latvian traditional culture has retained that model of emotionality, which is balanced and contained by reason.

Notes:

1 'Dainas'- short quatrains which are also referred to folk songs, but it is historically more precise to refer to them as 'dainas', as with the Norvegian 'stev'. The 'dainas' are occasionally compared to the Japanese haiku, in terms of the concentrated, laconic form of expression. The main difference is that haiku poems are attributed to a specific author.

2 With the reclaiming of Latvia's independence there is succeedingly greater influence from the West, and this has created some counter-reaction. For example, the 'Miss Latvia' contest instigated not only local contests for the most beautiful, but also most hard-working young woman.

3 V.Vike-Freiberga, *Cognitive Processes in the Perception of Art.* Nort Holland, 1984, 325-343.

4 H.Biezais - *Latviesu dainas ka kulturas vestures avots.- gr.;Smaidosie dievi un cilveka asara* (Latvian 'dainas' as a source of Latvian culture: The smiling gods and the human tears).Plone, 1991, 137.

5 This heading was attributed to the 'dainas' by one of the most legendary persons in Latvian culture- Kr.Barons-who was responsible for their collection and systematic compiling. This can be understood in light of the societal norms of the late 19th century and early 20th century, when sex was something which 'one could not speak of loudly'.

6 A.Millere. Women in Latvia: they endure all.- in: *Fragments of reality. Insights on women in a changing society.* Riga, 1992.,45.

Masculinity, Psychoanalysis and Politics

ANDREW SAMUELS

The roots of this paper lie in a number of recent political developments with which I have been closely involved. I have carried out a number of consultations with politicians in Britain and the United States designed to explore how useful and effective perspectives derived from psychoanalysis might be in the formation of policy and in new thinking about the political process. It is difficult to present psychoanalytic thinking about politics so that mainline politicians - for example, a Democratic Senator or a Labour Party Committee - will take it seriously. I have found that issues of gender and sexuality are particularly effective in this regard. Partly this is due to the perennial fascination and excitement carried by such topics. Partly it is due to the feminist politicization of such issues over the past thirty years which has gradually led to their presence on the agenda of mainstream politics. Partly it is because gender is itself a hybrid notion from a political point of view. On one level, in the social world of lived experience, gender and sexuality are everyday realities, suffused with experiences of power, powerlessness, vulnerability and misunderstanding. Gender has its own socioeconomic dimensions and set of electoral significances. But, on another level, gender is also an exceedingly private business as part of a story that people tell themselves and have told to them in attempts to produce, create or discover identities and relationships with others. Gender and sexuality are therefore liminal, sitting on the threshold between internal and external worlds, contributing to and partaking of both.

I have also been involved in the formation of three organizations whose objectives are relevant to the content of this paper. Psychotherapists and Counsellors for Social Responsibility is a professional organization, intended to facilitate the desire of many psychotherapists, analysts and counsellors to intervene as professionals in social and political matters making appropriate use of their knowledge and, it must be admitted, whatever cultural authority they possess. The second organization is a psychotherapy-based think tank,

Antidote. Here, the strategy has been to limit the numbers of mental health professionals involved so as to reduce the chances of psychotherapy reductionism and foster multidisciplinary work in the social policy field. Antidote has undertaken research work in connection with psychological attitudes to money and economic issues generally, and is also involved in work in the area of 'emotional literacy' but expanding the usual remit from personal relationships and family matters to include issues in the public domain. The third organization is a broad front based at St James's Church in London. The St James's Alliance consists of individuals from diverse fields such as politics, economics, ethics, religion, non-governmental organizations, the media, and psychotherapy. It attempts to incorporate ethical, spiritual and psychological concerns into the British political agenda and to facilitate a dialogue between non-governmental organizations, single issue groups and progressive political organizations. It is an experiment in gathering in political energy that is split up and dissipated under current arrangements.

It will be thought that psychotherapists and analysts such as myself are making these moves from an on-high and detached position, careless of the political issues affecting our own profession. However, all three organizations have been active in and profoundly affected by an acrimonious yet relatively successful campaign waged by elements of the psychotherapy profession in Britain to end discrimination against lesbian and gay men candidates for training in psychoanalytic psychotherapy and psychoanalysis. When psychotherapists get into politics they need to do so with a degree of consciousness over the appalling mess in which their own professional politics are usually to be found, as well as irony or even self-mockery over the counter-intuitive and slightly mad content of much of what they have to say.

Regarding a definition of politics, I have in mind an elastic one, ranging from conventional politics in Westminster, Brussels or Washington terms, to political struggles for resources and power, to a feminist-inspired reading of politics: the personal as political, the hidden politics of family life and relationships, and the politics of representation, cultural imagery and information.

These are three sets of questions that I am going to try to address, using 'masculinity' as a bridging element. First, where do new political ideas come from? How are they carried psychologically in culture? How do they spread? I am wondering if there is something to consider apart from the commonsense or obvious answers to those questions: that political ideas spread by word of mouth, by spawning organizations, by people's subversive reading of texts and so forth. But is there something else, for example, the idea of a political *Zeitgeist*, a political spirit of the time, that a psychological approach can flesh out?

One of my tentative answers to the question about how political ideas spread involves our getting a grasp on unconscious fantasies of incestuous sexuality that drive the relationships of what I want to call a man's *internal* family (to underscore the fact that I am not proposing that society is the family writ large). These fantasies and relationships, and what we think about them, may help in speculation about how political ideas are generated, how they transmit in culture and, to borrow a phrase of Stuart Hall's, how they have been 'sleeping in the public language' (Hall, 1974, p. 85).

The second set of questions concerns the divides that have opened up in modern political discourse between (a) ideology, (b) the social context in which ideology is produced, (c) the emotions that attach to ideology, (d) personal and emotional experience of living in the *polis*, (e) information about what is happening at a distance in society, and (f) political organization. My introduction of the portmanteau term 'political form' is a modest attempt to evaluate whether or not it is possible to bridge these divides.

My third set of questions reflects my interest in discussing the possibility of there being a progressive social role for therapy and analysis as a sort of think tank. For me, this role for therapy would depend on there being a progressive challenge mounted *within* psychotherapy to many of the conventional viewpoints and consensuses that exist. I do not think one can just take an ordinary set of well-known psychotherapy ideas (in this instance, about developmental psychology) and bang them into politics. One has initially to challenge the ideas that are current and common within psychotherapy, and then take the resultant mixture and move that in an indirect way into political discourse. There is no reason why this should be of any less 'practical' use than much of what constitutes contemporary sociology, political science or cultural studies in the academy. Perhaps the opposite is true if we see ourselves as, to some extent, held back from even partial fulfilment of political desires by restrictive and pessimistic self-conceptions and definitions of 'human nature'. Whilst I am sure that there are psychological (and economic and social and political) delimiters and constraints on political performance, process and thinking, I am not at all sure what they are. I do not see the apparent congruence between conventional psychoanalytical developmental psychology and current, existing political forms as somehow 'proving' that these are the only political forms that could - or even should - exist.

To summarize: I intend to dispute current, conventional and (in my view) one-sided readings of inner and outer relationships in which men participate by virtue of incestuous sexual fantasy. I hope to explore the sources and vehicles of new political ideas, to work the gaps between ideology, experience and organization, and to reposition the therapy room as a think tank.

Problems with this approach

There is undoubtedly a huge problem in mapping off from therapy onto society. A clear barrier exists between the individual psychological and collective/social levels of narrative, and maybe that barrier serves a useful function. Crossing it lightly might be dangerous in that psychoanalysis would seek to become a totalizing discourse, taking a position of mastery and normalization (see Samuels, 1993, pp. ix-xiii and pp. 3-23). For example, although my intention is quite the opposite, the undeniable fact that what I have written is within a Western cultural tradition, speaks to a certain extent of white male experience and places psychoanalysis in a more central and potent location than some others would, may lead critics to assert that I have universalized and normalized these variables. My belief is that work in transcultural psychology and psychotherapy points up the mutability of most of what psychoanalysis touches upon (see Samuels, 1993, pp. ix-xii and pp. 51-78). This actually strengthens the rhetorical strategy of the paper which is predicated on the changeability of *psychological* ideas as signifying part of the process of production of new *political* ideas.

Some would hold that the psychological and the social levels of reality are totally different and that, on a Marxist or neo-Marxist reading, the psychological may only be seen as a derivative stemming from hegemonic class forces which constitute a (or the) primary dynamic of the social. In similar one-sided vein, in the psychoanalytic tradition, there are those who would claim that psychic and social realities are indeed different from each other but that this is because the psyche (or the unconscious) uses projection to colour and cultivate the apparently external social world. Psychodynamics are primary. The social world is actually an ensouled world - *anima mundi*, soul in and of the world. Social and material aspects of our world, and the suffering to which they lead, are secondary phenomena.

Other thinkers, particularly in the past twenty years, have argued that there is a holistic oneness to be apperceived between the psychological and the social domains. It is an illusion to make these boundaries between psychological and social. Similarly, a holistic viewpoint goes on to maintain that the boundary between the inner and the outer is also illusory. Moreover, following the birth of ecopsychology (Roszak, 1993), it is being disputed, perhaps over-facilely, that we can maintain the epistemological boundary between the human and the non-human environments.

A dialectical approach would see psychological and social in ceaseless, unending, unsettlable, unclosable interplay, while a further possibility would be to say that the relations between the psychological and the social consist of *all* of the above. It just depends on the context, on who's talking, and on what he or she wants to do with these ideas. There would be no possible truth then; it would be, rather, a question of utility.

Finally - and this is the most challenging and difficult possibility - the relations between the individual/psychological and collective/social levels of reality, and the relevant discourses, might not be encompassed by any of the above approaches. There may be a missing bit in our psychopolitical thinking and vocabulary that, were it to exist, would help us to establish a new reading of the relations between the psychological and social, one that would not fall into the difficulties with all the readings that I have mentioned.

A further problem with the whole argument of the paper is that it courts danger because of the invocation of incestuous sexual fantasy. However, it is precisely because of the transgressive nature of incestuous fantasy (which, although involved therein, may be distinguished from actual incest, which is always destructive), that it is useful in thinking about and constructing what is frankly intended to be a transgressive politics. The whole point is to trade off and utilize the very anxiety that the kind of love represented by incestuous sexual fantasy rightly engenders.

Yet another problem is the risk that, when discussing parents, I have essentialized the parental function: mothers do this, fathers do that. I have taken some care not to essentialize parental function by grounding my work on the father in questions to do with lone mothers and with women parenting together (Samuels, 1995). A phrase with which I have become associated - 'the good-enough father of whatever sex' - is intended to make it very difficult for me, and indeed for anybody else, to offer hard-and-fast essentialistic comments on what it is that female parents do as compared to what it is that male parents do. Briefly, I have called women who parent alone or in relationship with other women 'good-enough fathers of whatever sex' because such women have to address what it is that fathers do or are supposed to do without the possibility of recourse to the traditional authoritarianism of male fathers when it comes to issues of discipline. There is a psychological sense in which the crisis in modern fatherhood and questions around lone parenthood - both perennially fascinating issues in most Western countries today - are the same issue. It is possible to reframe lone parents or lesbians parenting together as present-day experts on fathering.

Readers may wonder why I have focused so much on the male side, especially on the figure of the 'son' and not on the 'daughter'. Aside from practical issues of time and space, my interests are presently focused on the politics of masculinity - for example, male unemployment and what that is doing to male psychology in our time. One thing that interests me is the way in which what I call the 'male deal' is being busted by the discovery by many men - not just working-class men in rust-belt industries but also by middle-class men in white-collar and technical work - that they are not wanted any more just as they are and that they are going to have to learn all kinds of new skills. Young men are realizing that they face a life in which either they will never work, or they will have to learn, and relearn, and relearn again, different sets of skills and knowledge. The male deal is my term for the bargain that the average male in our society strikes with that society (one which has become of dubious advantage to many men).

In the male deal, a boy agrees to give up play, imagination, softness, fun, and an approach to life that is not goal-oriented - what is often called (although I really regret the term) the 'feminine' side of life - in order to have access to all the goodies that society can provide him with. I sometimes refer to this as 'all the woman you can eat'. This male deal has started to fall apart. Of course, inevitably, it is white, middle-class and middle-aged men who are challenging and questioning whether it was such a good deal for them in the first instance. But I think there are also certain ways in which the male deal, as I have just described it, is being challenged by other categories of men, with interesting and unforeseeable political consequences.

Incestuous sexual fantasy and new political forms

Let me move on to the connections between incestuous sexual fantasy and politics. Amongst other differences of opinion and personality, Jung and Freud split over the question of whether incest fantasies should be understood literally. For Jung, the images and symbols of incest in an individual carry a cultural meaning that goes beyond the circumstances of that person.

We usually approach incest in terms of pair relationships despite the fact that family therapists have noted the existence of incestuous patterns, atmospheres and systems in families. But what holds these pairs together in a family? For C. G. Jung, the answer to that question - what holds the pairs together in the family? - is 'kinship libido', which, to use his phrase, is like 'a sheepdog keeping the family intact' (Jung, 1946, p. 224). My further question concerns the role of kinship libido in society. Critically examined, can kinship libido be socialized, to be seen as that which holds social organisms and political forms together? If so, then different facets of kinship libido, different kinds of incestuous sexual fantasies, will be involved in the coming into being and the destruction of different kinds of political forms. At just one point, Jung hinted that kinship libido helps to hold 'creeds, parties, nations or states together' (Jung 1946, p. 233). Here we see enormous difference from Freud who, broadly speaking, identifies the need to protect culture and civilization from the incestuous components of Eros. Jung is arguing that kinship libido is the sheepdog that keeps an entire society intact.

A radical re-reading of highly charged love relationships in the family - sexually and politically charged relationships - can inspire new ideas about political forms, as well as helping us to analyze existing ones. Although psychology never wholly creates anything, I think it is usually implicated in politics at some level. To the extent that psychoanalytic psychology is built around sexuality and gender, those aspects of relations between persons in conventional and, in particular, unconventional families may be the most alive ways of factoring the psychological into political discourse.

So, what is a political form? I mean the existence of a unit of understanding and action within a society that combines the effects of ideology, narratives of emotional experience, and ongoing organizational structure. I see such a form as having a purpose or a goal, and also as having a much less tangible, more hermeneutic function. I think we talk about such things all the time when we talk about what kind of organization an institution or even a country is. We talk about an institution that is not a prison as if it were a prison. We talk about an institution that is not a madhouse as if it were a madhouse. We refer to places of work sometimes as families. And occasionally the phrase 'den of iniquity' will be used to describe a dry-as-dust organization that could not be further from being a 'den of iniquity'. What are we doing when we characterize organizations in this way? I think what we are doing is coming very close to speaking a language of political forms. We have a gestaltic image of the political form: its appearance plus its character plus our evaluation of it, all held together. The idea is to add something psychological to a materialist version of the social. Jacques Lacan may have had something similar in mind when, in the seminar of 21 January 1975, he displays a concern for form: 'Good form and meaning are akin' (Lacan, 1975, pp. 162-71). Lacan goes on to cite Charles Sanders Peirce on 'firstness' - what is it that divides things and signifiers into different qualities.

There are many uses of the term form in other disciplines. In biology, form means a variant type of life, something to do with the morphology, the shape, the bodily character of an organism. In philosophy the term form can mean the essential character of something. In social theory it means, loosely, organization. There are, if you trawl dictionary and thesaurus, some fascinating and suggestive additional meanings to the word form. Form can mean to train or develop something or someone. A form is a document with blank spaces to fill in. And a form is also a school bench.

There is something about social organisms that you cannot measure or assess accurately. The scientific fantasy breaks down. You can't weigh a political form or describe political forms in minute, empirical detail. This is true of a factory, a university, or an economic system. There is something about social organisms that it is very difficult to speak about with accuracy.

Another feature of form is that the same elements can lead to different forms. We learn this from biology, chemistry, and sociology. Now, if the same elements lead to different forms, isn't there something more than a material factor or set of factors to be considered? I am not interested here in eternal Platonic forms, or what one might call political archetypes. Nor am I following an Aristotelian path and saying that there are immanent political forms that are natural for political functions. Nor am I a nominalist, saying that political forms are just what I say they are, and outside of any discourse at all. Nor, clearly, I hope, am I mechanistic about it. What I am saying is that political forms involve psychological fields and are based to a great extent on incestuous sexual fantasy, what Jung called kinship libido. These psychological fields influence the creation, existence, and above all the mutability of political forms. But it is still a mystery how political forms come into being and change over time. There is no 'egg', there are no 'genes', in most visions of the social. But I think that there could be a place for a kind of social vitalism based on psychoanalysis. This would be on a politico-poetic level, if nothing else.

Vitalism holds that living organisms are organized by purposeful, mind-like principles. Teleology may be a dirty word these days, but even a materialist like Richard Dawkins uses its close neighbour, teleonomy, to link his Darwinism and the notion of final causes or purposes (1982). I would argue that there may be a purposive organizing principle in the social, which creates and destroys political forms, both ones that we approve of, and ones that we disapprove of. If this process is non-material in nature, then it can include human psychology.

Political forms are also concerned with the crucial role of in-form-ation. As I see it, we are dealing with fields of political information that derive their psychological shape from their location in relation to unconscious fantasies of incestuous sexuality and how these are managed in culture.

Explanatory note

Up to now, I have been preparing the ground for an exploration of four relations in a man's internal family: son-father, brother-brother, brother-sister, and son-mother. I shall follow the same pattern in connection with all four relationships. First, I will summarize the conventional wisdom about the problems and pathologies analysts and therapists seem to associate with these relationships. Then I will advance some different ideas intended to challenge the consensus. Finally, I will show how this thinking helps us to analyze existing political forms, inspires us to work towards new ones, and generally enhances our political self-awareness. There is a sense in which what looks like theory or even wishfulness is nothing more than description in words of what is already going on in many external as well as internal families, not to mention in many consulting rooms. In the human sciences, one often finds this state of affairs in which theory is truly an exposition of cutting-edge practices.

Son-Father

Scanning basic introductory texts in psychodynamics, psychotherapy and psychoanalysis, we see that the son-father relationship is said to involve castration, the question of the absent father, father as a role model for the son, father as a law-giver for the son, father as a moral presence, father as either successful or failing in separating the son from suffocating symbiosis with the mother.

I dispute this account, which tends to overlook the benevolent as opposed to the universally malevolent aspects of paternal sexuality. The notion of erotic playback between father and son (which is set out in Samuels, 1993, pp. 125-175) reframes their relationship in both bodily and political terms. Erotic playback takes place via a physically carried but symbolic communication that contains elements of admiration and even longing and yearning by the father in relation to his son; this is empowering for the son, and leads to what I call homosociality. (This term, suggested to me by Sonu Shamdasani, is one that Eve Kosofsky Sedgwick (1985) uses in a different context). Homosociality can be illustrated concretely by the way in which the gay community has responded to the challenge of HIV/AIDS, particularly when HIV/AIDS was thought to be a problem exclusively for homosexuals. So homosociality is already involved in a reframing of what we want from contemporary political organizations. But I am not only thinking about loving cooperation between men of different generations. I am also thinking of homosociality as inspiring a covenant of mutual protection between father and son in which they agree to look after, take care of, speak for, and protect the human rights of the other. However, in order for this covenant to come alive, father and son have to overcome the homosexual inhibition that our culture has placed so firmly at the heart of male identity.

Overcoming the homosexual inhibition moves us towards an apprehension of what male nurturing might look like and that itself would constitute an enormous challenge to most of the conventionally accepted ideas about the son-father relationship in psychoanalysis today. One aspect of this might involve what I call 'orientation melancholia'. This is a phenomenon I have met clinically in which a heterosexual becomes conscious of his depression over what he senses to be the lost opportunity of fulfilling his homosexual desires.

In a broadly similar way, the father's body is also a forum in which son and father work together on the transformation of aggression in its destructive and anti-social forms into a more socially creative kind of self-assertion. Aggression can never be eliminated as such but the movements within aggressive process can be tracked.

As regards new political forms that might stem from this particular set of ideas that I've been putting forward, and the challenge that they mount to conventional ideas, the most important locates cooperation as an element in political form, based on homosociality derived from erotic playback. Father-son cooperation based on a covenant forged in the heat of their bodily interaction and communication - hence involving incestuous sexual fantasy - I see as being primarily about cooperation and non-hierarchical relating between males rather than two males relating in tandem to an external object, such as football, or against a perceived threat, such as women. The move from boyhood to manhood involves more than an evolving recognition that one is not female.

One thing to note here is the absence, both in psychoanalysis and in culture, of a gay/straight dialogue about these things. Gay men know about the giving and receiving of bodily affirmation within an eroticized, loving context. Heterosexual men know less about it and here I think there is a very important political and psychological dialogue to consider.

Western societies have to engage with the whole question of valorizing homosexuality and homosociality (which does not mean idealizing homosexuality). It means making it more possible for heterosexuals to access the homosexual radical in themselves. I conduct workshops on new approaches to fathering, wherein everybody wants to be directly involved with children and to have a passionate, intense, responsible relationship with them. The biggest obstacle is that such aspirations bring up the fear of effeminacy. And effeminacy, in our world, brings up the spectre of homosexuality because male homosexuals are not proper men and hence must surely be women. And if male homosexuals are really women, then fear and loathing of femininity also kicks in. If new political forms are to come into being that could make use of the energies in new images of nurturing fathers, we will have to come to grips with our enormous fear of softness, effeminacy, and hence of homosexuality. Psychoanalysis needs to consider the prejudicial tendency in much of its theory to perceive male homosexuals as female- or mother-identified.

The male body has received political theorization mainly as a destructive presence in society. However, the supposed vulnerability of the male body, exemplified in current emphasis on men's health issues such as infertility and 'stress', may be one important plank in the construction of homosocial political forms. Male physical vulnerability is a form of male hysteria perhaps, less real than apparent, and mimetically linked to the roles of victim, underdog and abused one, imitative of women and children, in fact. It should not be allowed to obscure the sociopolitical realities of male power often mobilized in support of 'traditional' family roles, but, as Segal (1990) has shown, the very existence of a monolith 'men' is extremely dubious.

Brother-Brother

I will move on now to discuss the second of the four relationships, which is the brother-brother relationship. The conventional depiction of the brother-brother relationship is extraordinarily pathological. Nobody denies that it is a very important relationship, referring to Cain and Abel or Jacob and Esau - but tending not to mention Moses and Aaron (who did Moses's talking for him). The general consensus seems to be that there is something a bit odd about too good a brotherly relationship. Fraternity seems very close to pathology in psychoanalysis, as far as I can see. Everybody seems to be on firmer ground when the brother-brother relationship can be stated to be about rivalry, or the brothers depicted as receiving very opposite parental projections - if one is made into the thinker, then the other will be made into the doer. There is even a strand of imagery in the literature that suggests that the collective psychoanalytic association to brotherhood is rather bestial: we hear about top dogs, bottom dogs, and runts of litters. Finally, most texts on the brother relation do not stay with its particularity but move rapidly on to position the brothers in relation to the father (primal horde thinking).

My critique of this thinking is that psychoanalysis has pathologized away a necessary deep connection between men. This has been done by equating psychic growth and psychic health with absorption of the other, the opposite, the whole hetero-thing. We need to discuss whether health, or maturity, or growth always has to be in relation to something that is 'other'. The notion that we develop solely or mainly by absorbing, or relating to, or getting into a 'marriage' with the other is something that we get from society and culture, but I think that analysts and therapists have also promoted it. This is the typical pattern in which analysts and therapists are both reflecting the prejudices of a culture and contributing to those prejudices. Hence, if psychic health and growth, and, therefore, social health and growth are predicated on absorption of the other, then the brother-brother relation and brotherliness are ruled out of court as sources of health, whether on the personal or the political levels.

Perhaps it is time to resurrect the notion of the soulmate, but within a male frame. I am thinking of the social referents of warmth and closeness between men, homosexual as well as homosocial. We can think of this in terms of the particular psychology of the double and not solely in son-father terms. The idea is that psychological and social growth also rests on an encounter with the double. One example from Sumerian myth is the relationship of Gilgamesh and Enkidu, who appear in each other's dreams and, in the narrative, swap roles, one being bloodthirsty and out of control and the other rational and a good general and then vice versa. This kind of metaphorical brotherliness needs to be distinguished from brotherhoods - the locker room, old boys' network, Masons, Broederbund, secret society. Those well known, misogynistic bastions of male solidarity and power can be usefully understood as disavowals of or flights from the all-but-homosexual social and personal brotherly aspects of the brother pair. Brotherliness need not necessarily be anti-female. The role of the brother-brother relationship in male friendship patterns, and hence in political organization as a whole, is a topic about which very little has been written, although one meets with numerous spontaneous references to David and Jonathan. This contrasts with sisterliness and its role in female friendship and the sociopolitical organization of women.

Rethought in these ways, the brother-brother relationship may be seen as a template for a retheorizing of the anima. In Jungian psychology, the anima is the part of a man's psyche that connects him to his unconscious potential. Modern approaches to the anima see the female forms the anima takes as symbolizing what is 'other' to the man's consciousness (Samuels, 1989, pp. 92-106) rather than as indicating 'female' or 'feminine' characteristics. So it is altogether possible that a man's anima may appear to him (in projection) in the shape of another man and it is this possibility that I see as fuelled by my 'soulmate' reading of brotherliness (anima meaning soul). Apollo and Hermes are a further example: sibling gods who function as each other's anima. This is symbolized by the way they resolve their dispute over Hermes's theft of

Apollo's cattle: an exchange of gifts whereby Hermes gives Apollo his lyre, making him the god of music, and Apollo gives Hermes the aforementioned cattle.

What would new political forms inspired by brotherliness look like? What do we find if we analyze today's political forms with these thoughts about the brother-brother relationship in mind? For many reasons, there is a huge contemporary silence over fraternity. We still talk about liberty, and equality is continuously discussed. But fraternity has gone missing. The decline of trade unions is a significant feature here, illustrating the ways in which fraternity and political forms inspired by fraternity have slipped off the agenda. We are much more enmeshed in the politics of leadership and the models for leadership that we have inherited are paternal and heroic models with little place for the brotherly double.

The brother-brother relationship may well be a template for a different model of leadership. What would fraternal leadership look like? This is difficult to answer because most of us have little experience of such a paradoxical political form. It has not been much theorized. One example of leadership in a sibling vein comes from experience at a meeting of a witch's coven, a Wiccan group. Men can attend such covens. This particular coven made use of what they called a speaking stick. When a speaker had finished, she or he passed a staff to the person they had chosen to speak next. This replaced the more adversarial pattern of conventional meetings. Differences of opinion were introduced gradually and, over time, everyone present got to speak but within a different structure (or form) of communication.

Brother-Sister

Trawling the conventional texts, the stress is once again unremittingly negative. This may be something to do with the psychopathological project of psychoanalysis. But there may be other factors to consider given that jealousy, rivalry, mutual over-involvement and incest are the overwhelmingly predominant themes in relation to the brother-sister connection. I would like to propose that the central psychopolitical feature of the brother-sister relationship is that it concerns people who are equal in some ways but unequal in other ways, yet who are permanently connected or stuck together. It is different from marriage, though it might be part of a marriage, and not only as a problem for a marriage. We should heed with caution those marital therapists who condemn 'companionate' brother-sister kinds of marriages out of hand.

Some empirical research is useful here. A study was made of both what people applying to computer dating agencies wanted in their partner and what constitutes 'successful' relationships (Wilson and Nias, 1977). It seems from both sets of material that there is a general cultural awareness that, for a relationship to survive, there has to be a mixture of sameness and difference in it. Hence my suggesting that brother-sister relational dynamics may be much more useful in marital or cohabiting relationships than we have been led to believe.

There seems to be an omnipresent sociopolitical element in the brother-sister relationship, and most anthropologists have placed the brother-sister relationship and exchange at the centre of kinship systems. It's almost as if this relationship is screaming for someone to point out its Antigone-like political significance.

New political forms inspired by a rethinking of the brother-sister relationship would have to involve organizational recognition that there are irreconcilable antagonisms and prejudices between women and men. I am not persuaded by an idealization of man-woman relations in an image of them marching off together into a socially progressive sunset. I suggest that, in terms of political process, we need to stop thinking in terms of marriage or romantic love when it comes to men and women engaging in political actions. Instead, let us consider images of alliances, coalitions and deals between men and women when there are political purposes in mind. I think that the brother-sister relationship, as I have been depicting it, could be a psychological template for such a negotiatory approach to political organization, and to political forms that would rely on ambivalence-driven bargaining.

Observation of daughter and son has also suggested to me that there is something very important politically in the notion of a partnership between sister and brother against repressive parents. My children (and other children) do this well. They do not only struggle against each other. But something politically and psychologically destructive happens when the first of a brother-sister pair reaches the age of 10-11 years, just prior to puberty. Lively exchanges and mutual bantering and teasing - and the alliance against the parents that I have described - give way to mutual ignoring and a stand-off. What happens is more than the concrete result of their fear of incest. The mutual seduction of brother and sister certainly assists in the formation of a social bond against repressive parents. When culture smashes the structure of seduction between siblings, it also smashes the structure of resistance. Hence, in terms of political forms, anything that might deploy the brother-sister relationship as a twinning of difference and diversity is decidedly unwelcome. Psychoanalysis is uneasy about generational bonding against the parents on the basis of brother-sister erotics.

There is something also to consider here about the inevitable eroticization of political action. This is shown to good effect in Alexandra Kollontai's novel *Love of the Worker Bees*. She writes about what it is like to be in love during a revolution. Saying this is not to retreat into a Marcusian miasma. Rather, I merely want to point out that there is something in the brother-sister relationship, in addition to what is involved in romantic love or marriage, that would permit us once again to explore how exciting and meaningful it is on an erotic level for men and women to work together politically.

The brother-sister relationship may also be seen as a metaphor for the political forms arising from information technology and the Internet. I am thinking of the ideals behind the Internet, perhaps, rather than its inevitable, disappointing fate as part of someone's media empire. Such ideals include mutual learning, a non-hierarchical approach to communication, and a respect for indigenous knowledge. These are also the secret ideals of the brother-sister relationship which we could consider factoring into our attempts to construct new political forms.

Son-Mother

Conventionally accounts of the son-mother relationship may be summarized like this: 'You (the boy) must separate from your mother lest you fall into a female identification. Your mother is dangerous, seductive, and engulfing. You must not be a mother's boy. You must give up mother to father. You must give up mother to siblings. You must give up mother to her own destiny.' There is by now an alternative but equally conventional reading: 'You must harden yourself against the feminine. You'd better follow soccer. Take a stand against softness. Reject notions of play, imagination, and relatedness. You may not grow in connection.' This critique of masculinity is, of course, a feminist critique and, as I say, it has become a conventional alternative to the notion of a compulsory separation from mother brought about by the father but - this is an important point - even this reading is not usually taught on mainstream courses in analysis and psychotherapy, and hence its radical potential is unrealized in those contexts. It has stayed as a somewhat marginal feminist contribution to psychoanalytic psychology.

The following ideas of mind about the son-mother relationship are intended to challenge the conventional wisdoms about 'suffocating' mothers, 'possessive' mothers, 'Jewish' mothers, 'Mediterranean' mothers and the whole accusatory lexicon of mother-blaming. Do males have to separate from their mothers, as the books say they must? Do they have to slay the maternal monster? Do they have to be such heroes? Is this the only valid path of ego development? Is it possible to get beyond a situation where the son is required always to be an active and heroic man, and the mother is always depicted as a swampy, seductive maternal monster? Unfortunately, as Jung pointed out, 'the heroic deed of slaying the maternal monster has no lasting effects. Again and again, the hero must renew the struggle and always under the symbol of deliverance from the mother. Just as Hera, in her role of the pursuing mother, is the source of the mighty deeds performed by Herakles, so Nacomis allows Hiawatha no rest but piles up new difficulties in his path. The mother is thus the Daemon who challenges the hero to his deeds and lays in his path the poisonous serpent that will strike him' (Jung, 1911-12, pp. 348-9).

What if we were to recognize that both son and mother want to separate? What if this is the progressive *political* element in the psychological experience of maternal ambivalence, which, as Rozsika Parker has suggested (1995) aids creative maternal thought? Moreover, I think that if we apply what we know of context and contingency to the image of St George slaying the Dragon, which is the underlying cultural image behind Western science showing how the boy scientist dissects Mother Nature, we can recognize that this is not the only political form within which science can proceed. There is what has been called a feminization of science going on in which the epistemological relations between the exploring ego and its subject matter are being completely reframed, underlying the always already existing. These feminist-inspired new approaches to science (e.g. Keller, 1983; Rose, 1994) play into what I am proposing about reframing the son-mother relationship in a less adversarial way. We - not just we analysts and therapists - but we citizens need new images of the son-mother relation. In most classical mythology all great goddesses have a young male consort, and nothing seems odd or wrong about that at all. And does not Jesus in a way marry his mother when he symbolically marries the church?

Traditionally the theological and psychological question has been how to extract spirit (intellect, autonomy) out of the earthy mother's body and preserve it. I want to extract or discuss the politics from her relationship with her son. What would maternal leadership look like? Could a new version of the son-mother relationship give a more realistic basis for what is involved in the New Man phenomenon? And if there is going to be a new relationship of men to the environment to set alongside ecofeminism, doesn't there have to be a new reading of the son-mother relationship? Mother can symbolize earth as easily as earth can symbolize mother so the risk of demeaning essentialism is reduced.

Regarding political forms, what I have in mind here concerns the politics of protection and nurture and how these might be practised by others than mothers (and cf. Ruddick, 1989). We could identify political forms, based on and symbolized by the caring labour of mothers, which might lead us to discover the politics and psychology of the caring labour of sons, including to what extent sons could care for the sick and elderly, and involving models of nursing and teaching appropriate for sons. Such political forms would also recognize our ambivalent temptation to smash that which is vulnerable in the world, just as, according to Parker, every mother faces the temptation so to do.

A son-mother inspired political form could certainly involve nurture and imagination. But I think it could also be a political form that eschews or gives up power and striving altogether, performing an anti-heroic move in relation to politics. There might be a son-mother inspired politics of reflection and even of depression, a depression stemming from the loss of the privileged maternal relationship. It would be a pluralistic approach to political form based on the multifaceted tone of maternal experience. We are going to have to learn, we sons, how to have many mothers, just like Dionysus, who was variously mothered by Persephone, Demeter, Io, Lethe, Semele (cf. Hillman, 1973, p. 182).

In general terms, I want to reframe the son-mother connection as radical, son-friendly and fair, and as inspiring political forms that reflect those qualities. What do we come up with if we analyze today's political forms with these thoughts in mind? It is not a reassuring prospect. I realize there's a danger of idealization of the mother in what I'm saying and I do not think we could ever just stop seeing mother as swamp. The charge of idealization can also be countered by remembering that there will always be a fearsome maternal element to consider. In addition, changes in social and political practices (nurturing fathers, brotherly men, political siblings, mothers and sons who remain in connection) put pressure to change on the Symbolic Order. To the extent that analysis supports such changes, therapy, too, has a radical potential as a social and political practice.

Implications and concluding remarks

In this paper, I posed three questions. Where do political ideas come from, and what psychological vehicles carry them forward in culture? How do we evaluate the gaps between the effects of ideology, narratives of emotional experience, and ongoing political organizations that do or might exist? Is there a role for therapy as a kind of think tank? My tentative responses to my own questions incorporated the idea that therapy can function as a think tank if it interrogates its own conventional assumptions. The term political form was intended to be a way of linking ideology, emotional experience, and organization without reducing society to a family. Incestuous sexual fantasy, usually a transgressive property of the internal or external family, reworked in the ways I have been suggesting, leads us to envision and imagine new political forms. I suspect incestuous sexual fantasy has always done this or had the capacity to do this. Exploring such fantasies, deliberately restricting the scope of this paper to male fantasies and foregrounding the figure of the son, and looking into how they are thought and theorized by analysts and therapists offers an unusual and effective set of tools for examining, analyzing and even changing the political forms encountered in today's world.

In the son-father area of a man's internal family, I explored the implications for new political forms of a move from a focus on rivalry and castration to one on cooperation, mutual admiration and protection, and an acceptance and utilization of homosociality and homosexuality. This led to a discussion of cooperation and non-hierarchical organization and new forms of political leadership. One could envision significant changes in the political form of corporations and large institutions based on such ideas as a valorizing of erotic intimacy between men and an apperception of the vulnerability of the male body.

In the brother-brother area of a man's internal family, I explored the implications for new political forms of a move from a focus on complementary opposites falsely constructed by parents and the resultant competitiveness to an authentic recognition of differing abilities, brotherliness as a soulmate template for male friendship (as opposed to misogynistic brotherhoods), and the idea of the male anima. The changes in political forms this might inspire could include the reinstatement of fraternity as a sociopolitical and communal value or good, and the restructuring of the processes via which debate and dispute are carried out so that differences are introduced gradually. Brothers (citizens) would be seen as always already in relation to each other and not only to leaders or to centres of power (father and/or mother).

In the brother-sister area of the internal family of a man, I explored the implications for new political forms of a move from a fear of incest and a condemnation of brother-sister elements in 'mature' heterosexual sexual relationships to an acceptance of the seductive and ambivalent dynamics of the relationship as non-pathological. That led us to consider new political forms based on deals, alliances and partnerships between (metaphorical) brothers and sisters rather than on (metaphorical) marriages between husbands and wives of (metaphorical) romantic love affairs.

In the son-mother area of the internal family of a man, I explored the implications for new political forms of a move from a concentration on the satisfactory achievement by the son of separation from the mother and his formation of a 'hard' male identity to wondering if a developmental psychology could exist that was comfortable with mothers and sons who stay in connection. The mother would not be positioned as an abject and swampy enemy of the son's individuation but as an ally of the imagination, and the son would be more free to explore his taking on of 'maternal' roles in the family, in relationships and in society. Without idealization of the mother, new political forms could be theorized that would ground contemporary male aspirations of a politically progressive and humane kind, especially in relation to ecological consciousness, environmental politics, and economic and social justice.

References:

Dawkins, R. (1982) *The Extended Phenotype*. Oxford: Oxford University Press.

Hall, S. (1974) 'Deviance, politics and the media'. In *The Lesbian and Gay Studies Reader*, ed. Abelove, H., Barale, M. and Halperin, D. London and New York: Routledge (1993).

Hillman, J. (1973) 'The Great Mother, her son, her hero, and the puer'. In *Fathers and Mothers*, ed. Berry, P. Zürich: Spring Publications.

Jung, C. G. (1911-12) *Symbols of Transformation*. Collected Works Vol. 5. London: Routledge and Kegan Paul; Princeton, N.J.: Princeton University Press (1952).

Jung, C. G. (1946) *The Psychology of the Transference*. Collected Works Vol. 3. London: Routledge and Kegan Paul; Princeton, N.J.: Princeton University Press (1952).

Keller, E. (1983) *A Feeling for the Organism: The Life and Work of Barbara McClintock*, New York: Freeman.

Lacan, J. (1975) 'Seminar of 21 January 1975'. In *Feminine Society: Jacques Lacan and the École Freudienne*, Mitchell, J., Rose, J. (eds), Rose, J. (trans.), London: Macmillan (1982).

Parker, R. (1995) *Torn in Two: The Experience of Maternal Ambivalence*, London: Virago.

Rose, H. (1994) *Love, Power and Knowledge: Towards a Feminist Transformation of the Sciences*, Cambridge, England: Polity Press.

Roszak, T. (1993) *The Voice of the Earth: An Exploration of Ecopsychology*, London: Bantam.

Ruddick, S. (1989) *Maternal Thinking: Towards a Politics of Peace*. Boston: Beacon Press.

Samuels, A. (1989) *The Plural Psyche: Personality, Morality and the Father*, London and New York: Routledge.

Samuels, A. (1993) *The Political Psyche*, London and New York: Routledge.

Samuels, A. (1995) 'The good-enough father of whatever sex'. *Feminism and*

Psychology 5:6, pp. 511-530.
Sedgwick, E. (1985) *Between Men: English Literature and Male Homosocial Desire*. New York: Columbia University Press.
Segal, L. (1990) *Slow Motion: Changing Masculinities, Changing Men*, London: Virago.
Wilson, G. and Nias, D. (1977) *Love's Mysteries*. London: Fontana.

Love and Europe: Cultural Trends in the 1930s[1]

LUISA PASSERINI

This paper, an anticipation of a larger research, presents some points of an itinerary through the history of the discourses on love and on Europe which took place in some European countries, namely France, Switzerland, Britain, and Italy, in the 1930s. The gaps between these points - and between the authors discussed here -indicate that the present representation of the itinerary is incomplete, and the unexplored areas are large. Perhaps, however, this alternation of voices and silences can be suggestive of intellectual and emotional attitudes which belong to the past, but which it might be useful to re-consider in our age of Euro-scepticism and Euro-bureaucratism.

I. Finding Europe in the idea of love

At the end of August, 1933, a young Italian intellectual, Leo Ferrero, was killed in a car accident on a road of New Mexico. He had been on his way from Yale University (where he had spent a year working with a Rockefeller scholarship on the influence of Italian literature, following a sociology seminar led by Sapir) to China, Japan and India, where he was planning to study Oriental philosophy and to write a series of articles for the New York Times. When he died he was 30 years old, the son of two celebrities, Gina Lombroso, one of the first women in Italy to get a university degree (actually two, one in medicine and the other in literature), author of many books translated into various languages, and of Guglielmo Ferrero, sociologist and historian of international fame. The persecutions of the Fascist regime against his family had obliged Leo to migrate to Paris in order to pursue his career as a writer. His work was mainly literary, in the direction of writing plays for the theatre, short stories, a novel (lost), as well as critical essays on social and cultural themes.

In his published works as well as in his unpublished papers (especially the Carnets, which he kept as a diary) and in his private correspondence, Leo Ferrero developed an interpretation of love as the central aspect of civilization. Civilization was conceived as the way in which élites have coped with the problem of human suffering and found various solutions in order to face and stand it. Having been raised in a family composed of a non-practising Jewish mother, daughter of the great positivist scholar of criminal anthropology Cesare Lombroso, and a lay father, who was one of the most brilliant positivist thinkers and an antagonist of Benedetto Croce, Leo was not religious. There are some indications that in the last years of his life he was developing a sort of religious feeling and a non-confessional belief in God, but his conception is a lay one, based on principles derived from sociology and anthropology.

For Leo Ferrero, different civilizations have found ways of re-elaborating the excessive self-love that makes creation and production difficult, and induces so much suffering. Thus, love is interspered with civilization: 'l'amore s'è venuto intricando con la civiltà' (1929, Il muro). Among the solutions found by various élites he lists that by Christians, whom he equals with Europeans: they have deviated love from the self to God, while Hindus have drowned self-love and therefore individuality into the Universe (notes published by his mother in 1937 in the book Désespoirs). The type of love as passion that we know is, according to Ferrero:

> *a byproduct of christianism, the painful privilege of the west [sic]. I don't think - he wrote in April 1933, in one of his numerous love letters to many women, this one to an American lover - that Chinese and Hindus know what is passion. I don't think that the Roman and the Greek really knew it. [...] Christianism for the first time has freed the monster, has given a name to this mysterious force which was sleeping in the man, and has tried to direct it towards God. [...] When one has recognized in oneself the force and the need of love, if he cannot project it toward God, he will project it toward a human being. And passion is suffering, as it can be understood from the Latin meaning of the word, so that it is impossible to have passion and not to suffer. Dearest mine, I am still very tired and preoccupied.*

Within the same European civilization, according to Leo Ferrero, there are also relevant variations: the English, he wrote in 1929, have brought the limits of the self (moi) to the boundaries of their empire, and tried to placate the fury of self-love expanding it to an unlimited extension, so that love is not really present in English civilization and society. This is very similar to what takes place in Italian culture, for opposite reasons, i.e. because Italians have made of love the focus of individual life. In France love is the centre of social life, and is transfigured in such a way that social energies are conveyed into it, and it acts as a basis for cultural relationships and social manners. This is due to the capacity of French women to insert love into society rather than administrating only for themselves (Il Muro, p. 86: article of 1929 in Solaria).

It is too bad that these intuitions, based on Leo's father's and other social scientists' theories of élites, as well as on his own participant observation of love life in London, Paris and Florence, could not be developed. They remain in a mixture of common places and brilliant insights, such as the one on the narcissistic root of love, expressed in a fragmented form. Leo had inherited from his father, author of a famous book *L'Europa giovane* (1897), not only some sociological ideas but also a lively sense of being a European, strengthened by the experience of the narrow nationalism imposed on Italy by Fascism. A few years later in other countries more mature writers would express much more completely the intuitions that Leo Ferrero had on love in Western civilization. What was lost with him was on the one hand the lay perspective, the effort to understand love and its role outside a religious framework, on the other hand the refusal by Leo Ferrero to accept the link between love and marriage, dictated partially by this perspective and partially by his own psychological structure and his self-image, which could not envisage himself as a married person. His restless intellectual search had found a mirror in a series of suffered although reciprocated love relationships.

In the second half of the 1930s the development of an almost two-centuries old Eurocentric trend in romance philology was the basis for C.S. Lewis's interpretation of love in the European literary tradition. *The Allegory of Love*, 1936, was based on the assumption that the feelings sung by the troubadours of Provence and by the trouvères of Northern France at the beginning of our millennium had been the expression of one of the 'very rare real changes in human sentiments - there are perhaps three or four on record':

> *French poets in the XI c. discovered or invented, or were the first to express, that romantic species of passion which English poets were still writing about in the XIX [...] a sudden and revolutionary change that made the background of European literature for 800 years [and created] impassable barriers between us and the classical past or the Oriental present [...] compared with this revolution the Renaissance is a mere ripple on the surface of literature.*

If the Provençals (misnamed as French by Lewis) invented that type of love, the Italian poets, especially Petrarch, were the ones to refine it, but only the English poets, particularly Spencer, brought it to perfection, transforming the romance of adultery into the romance of marriage and contributing to the triumph of Christian values in the domain of love. In this perspective, the idea of Britain's mission to save Europe and its civilization finds a literary and imaginative expression. Reception of *The Allegory of Love* confirmed that the notion of a British leadership on this ground was welcomed by the critics. The Times Literary Supplement felt 'proud that English poets contributed so much to sanctify romantic love'. The belief of being the repositories of the highest form of love ever existed was challenged by only two out of about twenty reviewers: Harold Nicolson, who asked Lewis why he had ignored Sappho and the bucolic poets, and William Empson, who suggested Lewis to open The Tale of Genji (X c. Japan) as well as to read Islamic poetry and eventually The Song of Solomon.

The book by Lewis became a standard reading for a larger public than romance philologists, including university and college students, in whose formation it had an important role. Its success was permanent for decades, as it is still in print, without any change from the original edition of 1936. Therefore it finds its context not only in the specialized debate on the history of European poetry, but also in the cultural climate of interest for the South of Europe that developed in the period between the wars. In those years, the expansion of tourism made the Mediterranean an attractive place for an increasing number of 'children of the sun', and fostered the literary myth of certain Mediterranean areas as countries of love and romance. In this 'cult' the old Languedoc was included in a vaster area, Southern France and Italy, understood as places of origin of the European attitudes to love, where nordic people could regain their true selves (Fussell; Green). It was a step in the process of incorporation of the ideal of courtly and romantic love into a mass culture developing in films and literature.

In 1939 Denis de Rougemont presented his interpretation of the role of love in the Western tradition in *L'amour et l'Occident*, which was to become world famous and to have, as Starobinski wrote, 'an awakening power, resulting into a point of reference for the intellectual life of our century'. Starobinski's claim may sound exaggerated, but certainly L'A et O, translated into 15 languages and read by an educated not specialist public (as was the case with Lewis) in many countries over fifty years, has at the same time given words to diffused feelings and contributed to diffuse them.

Through an analysis of the myth of Tristan and Iseult, de Rougemont shows the emergence of a code of passion in Europe that combines influences from the East (from manichean and gnostic philosophies to erotic practices) with a typical Western tendency towards narcissism and death - through the exaltation of obstacles in love. Typical of the West would also become, in the course of time, the connection of passion with marriage, not present in the original myth. When the development of Western civilization eliminated all obstacles from love - as the growing rate of divorce showed, first of all in the United States, defined as a 'Europe without brakes' - and brought to the regimentation of sex through authoritarian eugenics (so that 'love between the wars became a curious medley of anxious intellectualism and of materialism', p. 267), politics transferred individual passions to the level of the Collective Being, the personified Nation, or the Party (268). The reference to Hitler's Germany is clear. To such a solution as well as to a freedom based on the emancipation of women and sexual mores in the USA, Rougemont counterposes the proposal of introducing the passion of faithfulness into marriage. On the basis of the philosophy of Kierkegaard and the theology of Karl Barth, he speaks of a troth which is observed by virtue of the absurd, by virtue of being an absolute which will uphold husband and wife as persons. Fidelity thus understood sets the person (see his *Politique de la personne*) and takes up an existential meaning on the basis of the unconventional nature of the troth.

Coherently with his whole work, in L'A et l'O de R. was trying to keep together the opposite terms of the dichotomies and fractures provoked by modernity. As he had done with cultural organizations, journals, groups, and the publishing house 'Je sers', he wanted to bridge the distance between protestants and catholics as well as orthodoxes and jews, between religious and not religious thinkers, between trade unionists and industrialists, between right and left (ni droite ni gauche), between hands and thought, as his book *Penser avec les mains* announced by its title. Rougemont was now trying to find bridges between East and West, marriage and passion, the one and the other, the man and the woman (one of the guiding lines in his research, inspired by Emmanuel Mounier, was: 'woman as a person'), in an effort that would not fuse or confuse the two, but, keeping their specificity and individuality, could establish a contact and a dialogue. The same type of conviction was at work in his federalism, that he extended from Switzerland to Europe: the attention being given to the local, the individual, through a decentralization that in the end rejoined the person and made a priority of it.

L'Amour et l'Occident, in spite of its historical and philological shortcomings, expresses a genuine sense of the spiritual crisis of intersubjective relations in Europe between the wars, in particular in the fields of love and marriage, and represents an answer in terms of existentialist philosophy and personalist theology that may not convince, but goes further than any simplistic form of moralism or libertarianism. The work by Rougemont provides a bridge also with the second trend of my research, and the second part of this paper.

II. Finding love in the idea of Europe

Contemporary with the trend of thought which I have been constructing under the title 'Europe in love', a sometimes parallel sometimes convergent trend existed, that I have named 'love in Europe'. Only a few people expressed both with equal strength: perhaps, if Leo Ferrero had lived, he might have worked out of his feeling of being deeply at heart a European, a form of passionate Europeanism. Rougemont certainly did establish the emotional roots of his post-war engagement in European politics in the interwar period. In 1932 he wrote in a piece by the title *L'intelligence est sentimentale*, included in the book *Paysan du Danube*:

> *Europe du sentiment, patrie de la lenteur- encore un paradis perdu! C'était bien notre dernier luxe, notre dernière gravité. [...] rien désormais ne pourra plus nous rendre le silence et la lenteur des choses. L'Europe des sentiments c'est notre Europe des adieux. Elle ne vit plus qu'en nous déjà, nous la portons encore comme le souvenir d'un soir d'adolescence.*

In 1943, writing from the US a short piece called *Mémoire de l'Europe*, he called Europe his 'patrie d'amour'. Together with this understanding of a Europe of emotions, he evolved the conception of a federalism centred on the experience of the country that he considered 'the heart of Europe', and abandoned the ambiguities towards fascism and nazism that had characterized the intellectual milieu of which he was part in Paris (l'Ordre Nouveau, the journal and group to which he had belonged published in November 1933 a letter to Hitler which stirred in 1934 harsh criticism from Emmanuel Mounier and Simone Weil).

De Rougemont's book *La part du diable*, written in the US and published first in 1942 then in 1944, analysed the collective responsibility of Europeans in the two world wars, requiring a prise-de-conscience of all forms of nationalism and totalitarianism. Hitler had been turned too quickly into the devil, without considering the devilish part that exists in democracy, i.e. the depersonalization connected with technology and modernity 'without a soul'. *La part du diable* confirms an interpretation given by Peter von Matt of *L'amour et l'Occident*, according to which Rougemont counterposes on the one hand the myth of vital space used by the Nazis and the myth of love claiming to have an absolute right to passion, to, on the other hand, respectively a democratic Europe, although denigrated and weak, and the alliance of marriage, also denigrated and weak.

Coherently with these trends of thought, in 1946 in Geneva de Rougemont formulated the idea of a union of European states as a first step towards a world federation:

> *il n'y a de Fédération européenne imaginable qu'en vue d'une Fédération mondiale. Il n'y a de paix et donc d'avenir imaginable que dans l'effort pour instaurer un vrai gouvernment mondial.*

Similar conceptions were held in England by the New Europe Group (NEG), founded in London at the end of the 1920s. It had connections with Ordre Nouveau, but it combined the idea of a united Europe with a strong interest for spirituality and esoterism. The group had developed out of the Adler Society founded in 1926 as the International Society for Individual Psychology, later transformed in name and nature in order to avoid Nazi attacks on its German members. The NEG brought together a number of people of very different intellectual origins, including eminent scientists, such as the botanist and town planner Patrick Geddes, the Nobel prize for chemistry winner Frederick Soddy, the monetary reformer Arthur Kitson, but also teachers, students, and professionals, around the figure of an extraordinary Serbian, Dimitrij Mitrinovic. Mitrinovic developed a syncretism of political ideas and an interpretation of the spiritual needs of the epoch which combined the psychoanalysis of Adler with the philosophy of Auguste Comte, the religious thought of the Russian Vladimir Solovyov, as well as elements from Nietzsche, Otto Weininger, Maz Stirner and Rudolf Steiner.

According to Mitrinovic, Universal Humanity could be achieved only through the conscious will of free individuals. It was in Europe, in the Western world that, under the influence of Christianity, individuality and reason were most developed and valued; therefore, in order for the world to be organized as an organic whole, it was Europe that must take the lead. This was not to say that Europe had a right to rule and determine the course of the world in pursuance of her narrow interests, which had already produced the 'crimes' perpetrated by Europeans on the Black race and on China, in 'an almost unbroken story of chicanery, greed and ill-will'. But Europe's relations 'with the Black as well as with the Yellow race have been largely instinctive, not specifically European', because 'Europe as a cultural entity has not yet been developed'. The stress here is on the future rather than on the past, a feature which distinguishes this position from many other ones on European identity, and nuances its Eurocentrism.The Federation of Europe, the synthesis of Europe, is the primary condition of the Alliance of Humanity, of a world-synthesis.By 'synthesis' Mitrinovic meant a spiritual and cultural vision which should inform the future unity. His Europe included Russia, the Balkans, Britain, the mediterranean countries, not to be united simply on a political or military basis. The task before Europe was to create an all-inclusive European culture, as a preliminary way not to imposing it to the world, but to maintaining it as the world's standards of reference. Europe must be worthy of the world's reference of values. Mitrinovic was calling in the first instance for New Europeans rather than for a New Europe. The failure of the NEG to create a political movement was in good part due to his refusal to reduce to a party what he believed to be the spiritual task of the age.

The opposite call, by Goebbels, to a 'Europe of the future' dominated by Nazism, coupled with Goebbels's theory of total war, smashed the hopes of the British NEG. Their call to a spiritual and psychological regeneration, and to a redefinition of intersubjective relations between individuals and peoples, had to give way, in presence of extremely violent confrontations on the continent, to an armed Resistance that opposed to fascism and nazism the effort to save whatever was left of Europe.

In the summer of 1941 a few Italian antifascists, confined in the island of Ventotene, wrote the Manifesto for a free and united Europe. They belonged to the Liberal Socialist movement founded in Paris in 1929 by Carlo Rosselli, Emilio Lussu, Gaetano Salvemini: Giustizia e Libertà, later to give rise to the Partito d'Azione. In Ventotene were Ernesto Rossi, Eugenio Colorni and his wife Ursula Hirschmann (a socialist who had been obliged to leave Berlin as a student), and Altiero Spinelli, who in 1937 had left the Italian Communist party because of Stalin's crimes, and who wrote materially the Manifesto. Through the action of Ursula Hirschmann, a clandestine publication, Europa unita, diffused their ideas. In August 1943 a Movimento Federalista Europeo was founded in Milan and the following year an international clandestine meeting was held in Switzerland. After 1944, when her husband Colorni was killed in the Resistance, Ursula Hirschmann married Spinelli; they both became Europeanist activists and in the 1970s she founded in Brussels the association Femmes pour l'Europe.

While Europeanism was a total passion for both Ursula and Altiero, in that passion there was certainly something of their reciprocal love. Ursula had written of her previous marriage:

From falling in love with his ideas (Colorni's, who had criticized her mechanistic Marxism) to falling in love with him, it was a short way, almost a necessary way. I could not imagine to live far away from that source of ideas, always new, original, moving ideas. I owed Eugenio the access to that free space [...] in a dialogue that continued throughout our difficult life together and even after our separation

Ursula Hirschmann expressed vividily the dramatic contradictions of many women's access to the world of political and theoretical discourse, the deceiving role of emotions, the mystifying connection between love and politics. However, she kept her faith in both love and politics, perhaps also thanks to the fact that a much deeper understanding, not so intellectualistic, was at the basis of her second marriage. She considered herself a 'wandering European', without a language, not Italian in spite of having Italian children, not German even if Germany had been her fatherland. In *Noi senza patria* (we without a fatherland), an unfinished collection of her writings, she wrote, echoing and transforming Marx: 'we are federalists because in a united Europe we have nothing to lose but our chains'.

The emotional basis of this idea of Europe is linked with something that I would like to call an active memory of emotions, capable of continuing but re-elaborating the legacy of national cultures into an international perspective, the legacy of Marxism and of its struggles against social injustices, and vitalized through a contact with a liberal radicalism capable of freeing that legacy from the rigidity of schemes. In this active memory, the role of 'a city called Europe' is essential; this echoes de Rougemont, but in a less nostalgic tone: in Ursula's words, it is a 'city that I have in myself'. Ursula Hirschmann seems to be very aware of the fact that there is no real memory without an emotional basis, and that any active work of elaboration of ideas, theoretical as well as political, requires a high libidinal investment. For her the emotional roots find their ground not only in individual and collective memories, but also in art and in local places which are the homes of the 'small':

We can only love. Not because we are good, not because we are religious, but because it is our only way to remain in reality. Because Moerike [with his beautiful poems closed in a world as small as a nutshell] is always there and no Eichman can take him away from us.

These words were written some years later, between 1957 and 1974. They were still unspoken but perhaps had already nourished the drier words that composed the Manifesto of 1941: a federation of European states with a central government elected by the peoples of the member states, with a constitutional supreme court, with a federal army substituting the national armies, with the structures necessary to enforce in the single states a common order compatible with local autonomies.

Epilogue

The itinerary that we have followed has started with an Italian who worked in London and Paris and died in the US, has continued with an Irishman who worked in England and married an American, then with a Swiss who lived in Paris and New York, with a Serbian who lived in London keeping important contacts with Central and Eastern Europe, with an Italian and a German who fought in Brussels for a different idea of Europe than that which was being constructed there in the second post-war period. By their own lives these intellectuals show the interconnectedness of European and Western culture. They nourished feelings and ideas that were consciously accepted by minorities, sometimes extremely small ones (but not always), and expressed some subterranean trends destined to be consciously shared only much later on.

Their works provide a very diverse range of values and fields of engagement, and are marked by the times and conflicts they lived through. Their ideas were, to various extents, riddled with eurocentrism and ethnocentrism; they were also, in spite of the conscious efforts by some of those people, such as de Rougemont and Mitrinovic, largely male centred, being part of a culture that had been subjected to a gender critique only in some of its aspects. At the same time in recent decades, the idea of a spiritual and emotional regeneration has migrated far from the connection with Europeanness, and the idea of a European specificity of love has ceased to be a central core of identity. Anthropological research tells us that forms of romantic love have existed in many cultures, from Australian aboriginal communities to the People's Republic of China (Jankowiak), where it has dictated poetical expressions, songs, tales, and informed personal relationships.

However, in the European authors we have encountered, there were directions of thought which could be of use in a multicultural and universalistic perspective. More precisely, two aspects that could be extracted from the cluster of ideas, attitudes, and feelings that we have been revisiting, are: 1, the connection between identity and emotion, and 2, the inclusion in intersubjectivity of both distance and closeness. While the feelings called romantic love were not unique of European civilization, there has been in Europe, more discernible than elsewhere, a contradictory tendency to develop those two aspects as well as their interconnectedness. Today these two do not belong to Europe any longer, but to a world dimension of intersubjective relations. Clearing up the contradictions, also through historiographical work, might contribute to understand, value and develop those forms of interconnectedness and intersubjectivity.

Notes:

1 Versions of this paper were given in seminars at the European Institute in Florence, the Institut für die Wissenschaften vom Menschen in Vienna and at the Humboldt Universität in Berlin. I thank all those who made comments and posed questions on those occasions.

References:

Ferrero Leo (1984): *Il muro trasparente* (edited by Manuela Scotti), Quaderni della Fondazione Primo Conti, Scheiwiller, Milano.

Fussell Paul (1980): *Abroad. British Literary Traveling Between the wars*, Oxford University Press.

Green Martin (1992): *Children of the Sun*, Pimlico, London.

Hirschmann Ursula (1993): *Noi senza patria*, Il Mulino, Bologna.

Jankowiak William (ed.) (1995): *Romantic Passion. A universal experience?*, Columbia University Press, New York.

Kornfeld Anne (1993): *La figura e l'opera di Leo Ferrero*, Gutenberg, Povegliano Veronese.

Lewis C.S. (1987): *The Allegory of Love*, Oxford University Press, Oxford 1936.

Mitrinovic Dimitrije (1995): *Lectures 1926-1950*, New Atlantis Foundation in association with J.B.Priestley Library, University of Bradford,
(1987): *Certainly, future*. Selected Writings East European Monographs, Boulder, New York.

de Rougemont Denis (1939): *L'amour et l'Occident*, Plon, Paris 1939;
(1945): *La part du diable*, Neuchatel.
(1995): Le paysan du Danube et autres textes, L'Age d'Homme.

von Matt Peter (1989): *Liebesverrat. Die Treulosen in der Literatur*, Muenchen.

List of contributors

Dagmara Beitners is historian of religion and assistant at the Institute of Philosophy and Sociology at the Academy of Sciences in Riga, Latvia

Emilios Christodoulidis is lecturer at the Centre for Law and Society, Faculty of Law at the University of Edinburgh, Scotland

Marie-Claire Foblets is professor of immigration law at the Catholic University of Leuven in Belgium

Saxo Grammaticus lived about 1200 A.C., and was a Danish/European historian who wrote Gesta Danorum

Niels Henrik Holmqvist-Larsen is a Danish historian and a specialist on the medieval European historian Saxo Grammaticus

Luisa Passerini is professor of history at the European University Institute in Florence, Italy

Hanne Petersen is professor of law and legal sociology at Ilisimatusarfik, University of Greenland, Nuuk, Greenland

Koen Raes is professor of legal philosophy at the Department of Legal Theory, Legal Philosophy and Applied Ethics at the University of Ghent in Belgium

Andrew Samuels is practicing analyst, political consultant and professor of analytical psychology at the University of Essex, England

Thomas Spijkerboer is lecturer in Migration Law at the Centre for Migration Law, University of Nijmegen, the Netherlands

Ditlev Tamm is professor of legal history at the University of Copenhagen, Denmark